About Pearson

Pearson is the world's learning company, with presence across 70 countries worldwide. Our unique insights and world-class expertise comes from a long history of working closely with renowned teachers, authors and thought leaders, as a result of which, we have emerged as the preferred choice for millions of teachers and learners across the world.

We believe learning opens up opportunities, creates fulfilling careers and hence better lives. We hence collaborate with the best of minds to deliver you class-leading products, spread across the Higher Education and K12 spectrum.

Superior learning experience and improved outcomes are at the heart of everything we do. This product is the result of one such effort.

Your feedback plays a critical role in the evolution of our products and you can contact us – reachus@pearson.com. We look forward to it.

Praise for *The Business Model Book*

'To build a great business, you need a powerful business model. This book gives you all the tools to make it happen. Clever, innovative, and simple – a must read workbook for entrepreneurs!'

Charles CHEN Yidan, co-founder, Tencent Holdings

'A rich compendium of everything you need to know about business models – and more! The frameworks, exercises and examples build essential skills for anyone considering starting or rapidly growing a business. Buy it. Read it. Most importantly, use it!'

John Mullins, London Business School; author, *The Customer-Funded Business* and *The New Business Road Test*

'Gets you thinking on what value you deliver as a business and how you deliver it. This may well turn out to be your scrapbook for business models. An excellent resource that will get your ideas flowing!'

Shane Corstorphine, VP, Regional Growth (Global Regions) and General Manager (Americas), Skyscanner

The Business Model Book

The Business Model Book

Design, build and adapt business ideas that thrive

Adam J. Bock
Gerard George

Pearson

Original edition, entitled *The Business Model Book: Design, Build and Adapt Business Ideas that thrive,* 1st Edition, by Bock, Adam J. and George, Gerard published by Pearson Education Limited, Copyright © 2018.

Indian Subcontinent Reprint

ISBN 978-93-534-3000-9

First Impression, 2019
Fourth Impression, 2024
Fifth Impression, 2025

Published by Pearson India Education Services Pvt. Ltd, CIN: U72200TN2005PTC057128

Head Office: 1st Floor, Berger Tower, Plot No. C-001A/2, Sector 16B, Noida – 201 301,Uttar Pradesh, India.

Registered Office: Featherlite, 'The Address' 5th Floor, Survey No 203/10B, 200 Ft MMRD Road, Zamin Pallavaram, Chennai - 600044
Website: in.pearson.com; Email:companysecretary.india@pearson.com

Digitally printed in India by Trinity Academy for Corporate Training Ltd, New Delhi in the year of 2025.

Dedications

Adam

This book is dedicated to my wife, Lynn Hyland, who always feared I had another book in me. Three books, two kids and a cat: I think the family is big enough now. Her love and support has made all the difference.

'Being a woman is a terribly difficult trade since it consists principally of dealings with men.'

Joseph Conrad, *Chance*

Gerry

To my wife, Hema, and my girls, Vivian and Maegan.

Adam and Gerry

This book is also dedicated to all the entrepreneurs who took irreplaceable time from their personal and professional journeys to share their stories. We are constantly reminded of the courage and perseverance of entrepreneurs around the globe, especially those who combine inspiration, hard work and altruism to make the world a better place.

'What recommends commerce to me is its enterprise and bravery. It does not clasp its hands and pray to Jupiter. I see these men every day go about their business with more or less courage and content, doing more even than they suspect, and perchance better employed than they could have consciously devised.'

Henry David Thoreau, *Walden*

Contents

Acknowledgements

This book owes its existence to a variety of people and institutions. We are grateful to the Pearson team. Steve Temblett got the project started and Eloise Cook made sure the book was completed.

Adam
Professor Anne Miner at Wisconsin provided invaluable wisdom on life and learning. Professor Nick Oliver hired and supported me at Edinburgh. Professors Amy Gannon and Mark Barnard welcomed me to Edgewood College.

Hundreds of entrepreneurs have shared their stories with me – if I started naming them I wouldn't be able to stop. Organisational scholars are lucky to find willing research subjects. My thanks to the business people who have provided mentorship and friendship over the years, including Tom Terry, Paul Reckwerdt, José Estabil, Larry Landweber, Joe Boucher, Charles Neider, Phil Blake and many, many others.

To the extent I have been successful as an academic and business person, I owe a significant amount of that success to these and other colleagues, friends and family.

Gerry
Academic life is a journey – and, on every step, I was fortunate to have had the support needed to get through to the next mile marker. Whether Singapore, London, Madison (Wisconsin), Syracuse (New York), Richmond (Virginia) or Chennai (India), I have benefitted from the largesse of colleagues, students,

co-authors, business partners, friends and family. I am deeply indebted and ever so grateful. Thank you!

I'd like to thank The Lee Foundation, Singapore, for its generous support to my professorship and the Lee Kong Chian School of Business at Singapore Management University.

Publisher's acknowledgements

We are grateful to the following for permission to reproduce copyright material:

Figures
Figure 10.1 adapted from https://blog.leanstack.com/why-lean-canvas-vs-business-model-canvas-af62c0f250f0; Lean Canvas is adapted from The Business Model Canvas (http://www.businessmodelgeneration.com) and is licensed under the Creative Commons Attribution-Share Alike 3.0 Un-ported License; figure 11.1 adapted from https://strategyzer.com/canvas/business-model-canvas; this work is licensed under the Creative Commons Attribution-Share Alike 3.0 Un-ported License; figure 14.1 adapted from Agile Business Model Innovation, The European Business Review, May/June 2014 edition (Adam J. Bock and Gerry George, 2014), first published in *The European Business Review*, http://www.europeanbusinessreview.com/agile-business-modelinnovation/.....; figure 15.1 adapted from http://www.plan-c.eu/bmix/, source: Circular Flanders, Reproduced with permission.

Text
Case study on page 31 reproduced with permission from Vash Marada; quote on page 117 from Thomas Whiteaker, Partner, Propel Venture Partners, Personal interview with Adam Bock, Reproduced with permission; quote on page 34 from John Biondi, interview with Adam Bock, Reproduced with permission; newspaper headline on page 40 from Esther

Dyson, https://www.linkedin.com/pulse/20130722164610-28157-hyperloop-it-s-the-business-model-stupid, Reproduced with permission; quote on page 95 from Mark Daugherty, Serial entrepreneur, Personal interview, 2015 with Adam Bock, Reproduced with permission; extract on page 96 adapted from http://www.shortstackeats.com/, Reproduced with permission; extract on page 120 from Value Creation vs. Value Capture by Marty Cagan, 21 April 2013, https://svpg.com/value-creation-vs-value-capture/, Reproduced with permission; quote on page 140 from Ash Maurya, https://leanstack.com/why-lean-canvas/, Reproduced with permission; quote on page 238 from John McKinley, former CTO at Merrill Lynch (personal correspondence), Reproduced with permission.

About the authors

Adam J. Bock is an entrepreneur, executive, academic and financier.

Adam is the co-founder of four life science companies spun out of university research. Nerites Corporation was purchased by Kensey-Nash (Royal DSM) for $20 million in 2011. Stratatech Corporation was acquired by Mallinckrodt in 2016 for $187 million. Virtual Incision Corporation is actively commercialising miniaturised surgical robots. His most recent venture, Cellular Logistics, was spun out of the University of Wisconsin in 2016. Adam has managed multiple angel investing networks, facilitating more than $10 million of seed investments into early stage technology firms. He mentors technology and social entrepreneurs around the world.

As an academic, Adam studies technology entrepreneurship, business models, technology transfer and sustainable entrepreneurship. Adam is the co-author (with Gerry) of *Inventing Entrepreneurs* (Pearson Prentice Hall 2009) and *Models of Opportunity* (Cambridge University Press 2012), and has published articles in *Entrepreneurship Theory and Practice, Journal of Management Studies, Venture Capital: An International Journal of Finance, The European Business Review* and other journals.

He has taught entrepreneurship at the University of Wisconsin-Madison, the University of Edinburgh, Imperial College London, Skolkovo Institute for Science and Technology and Edgewood College. He holds Bachelor's degrees in Economics and Aeronautical Engineering from Stanford University, an MBA from the University of Wisconsin-Madison and a PhD in Innovation and Entrepreneurship from Imperial College London. He is a Fellow of the UK Higher Education Academy and a Member of the Royal Society of Edinburgh Young Academy.

Adam lives in Madison, Wisconsin (USA) with his wife, Lynn Hyland, and their two children, Taran Lee and Kenna Rose. Adam's real day job is to thwart his children's plan for world domination at the behest of their cat overlord, Phoenix. The business model of Kenna's start-up company, Exvarderus™, is obviously just a front for this evil scheme.

Gerard (Gerry) George is dean and Lee Kong Chian chair professor of innovation and entrepreneurship at Lee Kong Chian School of Business at Singapore Management University (SMU). Gerry joined SMU from Imperial College London, where he was deputy dean of the Business School, director of the Gandhi Centre and academic director of the London Stock Exchange's ELITE Programme, which supports ambitious private companies through their next stage of growth. Before Imperial, he held tenured positions at London Business School and at University of Wisconsin-Madison.

An award-winning researcher and teacher, Gerry has published over 100 articles in leading scholarly journals. From 2013 to 2016, he served as editor of the *Academy of Management Journal,* the flagship empirical journal in the field of management. He was awarded a prestigious Professorial Fellowship from the UK's Economic and Social Research Council to work on resource-constrained or inclusive innovation. His research investigates business models, organisational design and its implications for innovation and entrepreneurship. His books (with Adam) introduce a narrative approach on how entrepreneurs conceive and change business models to make an implausible idea into a viable growth opportunity, *Models of Opportunity: How Entrepreneurs Design Firms to Achieve the Unexpected* (Cambridge University Press 2012) and *Inventing Entrepreneurs: Technology Innovators and their Entrepreneurial Journey* (Pearson Prentice Hall 2009) addresses the human side of innovation and technology commercialisation.

He serves on the board of the Association to Advance Collegiate Schools of Business (AACSB) International. The AACSB is the world's largest business education network connecting students, academia and business to advance business education worldwide. Founded in 1916, AACSB is a global association of more than 1,500 member organisations in over 90 countries and territories, with headquarters in North America, Asia Pacific and Europe. Gerry also serves on the Board of Governors, and in an honorary role as International Dean, of BML Munjal University, near New Delhi. Previously, he served as a non-executive director and chaired the Risk Management Committee of India Infrastructure Finance Company (UK) Limited (IIFC), a Government of India enterprise subsidiary. IIFC (UK) provides dollar denominated financing for capital equipment in large Indian infrastructure projects such as power generation, urban mass transit and ports, amongst others. For his contribution to further education and research, Gerry was awarded Fellowship of the City & Guilds of London Institute.

Foreword

As I read this book, I thought back on my entrepreneurial career. Across 30 years and the five companies I've started and run, I never once thought about business models.

My second company, TomoTherapy, probably did not need a lot of business model analysis. It was driven by our passion to cure previously untreatable cancers. Perhaps we were smart; perhaps we were lucky. Regardless, TomoTherapy has saved thousands of lives and generated wealth for the founders and employees.

But as I worked through the examples and worksheets in the book, I realised how much I could have used this – for my own startups, the ventures I've funded and the entrepreneurs I've mentored.

Anyone who has run a company, successful or not, recognises the critical relationships between customer, supplier, personnel, resources, funding and the dream. This book gives you a framework to visually design and evaluate that dream. It will show you the huge gaps that you will have to fill!

Just be totally honest when you do this. Don't fool yourself, my friend.

I agree that there are millions of business models but most fall into just a few categories. If you are trying to insert yourself into a well-established industry, then figuring out your competitors' business models will be essential. Before you spend tons of money and time, you can assess whether you really do have the key to slip in and stomp them.

At TomoTherapy, we were attacking an entrenched, somewhat ossified industry. I had intuitively assessed the dominant business model and saw the huge holes in it. That business model had worked for years, decades even. Its success made the key players cavalier and dismissive. Dissatisfied, frustrated customers wanted alternatives. We launched a new technology with a different vision. That gave us a new business model and a great opportunity.

But if I had this book early on, I would have started with a better model for my other ventures. That would have saved me at least one or two face-plants and near collapses.

Something to keep in mind, however, is that a brilliant business model can very quickly turn into a bad business model. A fast growing company changes dramatically and your relationships evolve day to day. Customers, markets, competitors, and industries can shift, sometimes very rapidly. I really like that Adam and Gerry advise you to see business model analysis as a cycle. You return to it regularly to check the validity of your data, your assumptions and your narrative. If you don't, you are probably just fooling yourself after all.

Don't be afraid of change; it is the key to staying viable. Just work through the cycle and the analysis to see if you are missing something. After all, you want to know now whilst you can still change, before it's too late.

This book may be simple to read, but there are lots of gems in the frameworks, analysis and worksheets. Besides the structured approach to designing your dream, the examples and comments are priceless to an entrepreneur. Adam and Gerry may be academics, but they've also been entrepreneurs.

Their knowledge is based on rigorous research and hard-won practice.

There are many things successful entrepreneurs learn by trial and very painful error. Tap into these lessons: take advantage of this unique opportunity to learn from our mistakes. Keep your model and this book around for reference in the future. Believe me, it will help you sometime, somewhere.

Paul J. Reckwerdt
Founding CEO, TomoTherapy
Madison, WI

Brief notes on the text

We have tried to make this book clear *and* concise. This required certain compromises. Scholarly research, novel technologies and new business models often cannot be comprehensively explained in a few paragraphs without oversimplification. The authors assume that interested readers will follow up on specific topics in more detail at their leisure.

To avoid 'academese' and maintain the flow of the text, we have not used in-line citations or references. We have created a website for the book (www.thebizmodelbook.com) that includes a variety of useful resources. We encourage every reader to access the worksheets, which provide an opportunity to 'DO' rather than just 'ABSORB'. The website also provides extensive links to articles and references on the web, a lengthy set of 'Excursions' for inquisitive readers who would like more insight into certain topics and even tangential discussions that we thought were interesting but couldn't be included in the main text. The website also includes a very limited bibliography of academic and practice-oriented books, papers and resources. The simple reality is that the availability of Google Scholar and other searchable systems make such a bibliography a bit redundant, but it is included for two reasons. First, we wanted to recognise some of the published work that has most influenced our thinking as academics. Second, we wanted to provide a reasonable starting point for readers less familiar with the academic and practice literatures on business models and related topics. We are both concerned and amused that rigorous organisational research is commonly unreadable to everyday managers and entrepreneurs. Perhaps this, too, is an opportunity for business model innovation.

For information about gender language and semantics of the word 'entrepreneur', please see the Entrepreneurial Language Excursion on the book website. For information on our approach to cases and examples, please see the Cases and Examples Excursion.

How to use this book

You may use this book purely for information or even entertainment, simply by reading it straight through. It is designed, however, as a *workbook* for entrepreneurs, managers and executives.

Each chapter has specific examples and activities designed to apply business model thinking to a specific situation. You can learn a lot from the examples and the general explanations. If you want to make a difference at your organisation, then you should think carefully about the stage of your business and complete at least the activities appropriate to that stage.

Completing all of the activities provides the most insight – even the ones that may not seem relevant to your business. Companies change over time and *so do business models.* For example, trying out the growth stage business model activities for a start-up may seem to be putting the cart before the horse; however it is quite likely you will see key elements of your longer-term business model in advance. Alternatively, if you have the opportunity to rapidly scale your business in the future, you will be able to look back and think about your original assumptions. Are those assumptions still valid?

This book is accompanied by a website:

www.thebizmodelbook.com. At this site, you will find:

- Worksheets that can be downloaded for your own use.
- Links to the examples and resources mentioned in the book.
- 'Excursions' that cover related topics that might be of interest.
- Further readings, including books, popular media and scholarly publications.

Give it a try. After all, you are reading this to learn something. As with entrepreneurship (and life), you will probably learn it best by doing it.

Introduction

In a world of buzzwords, 'business model' may be the biggest buzzword of all.

Figure 0.1 shows how mentions of 'business model' have outpaced other key management concepts in the past decade. Even as some other key management tools and ideas fade, the business model gains wider use and attention from both practitioners and researchers. It appears the business model is here to stay.

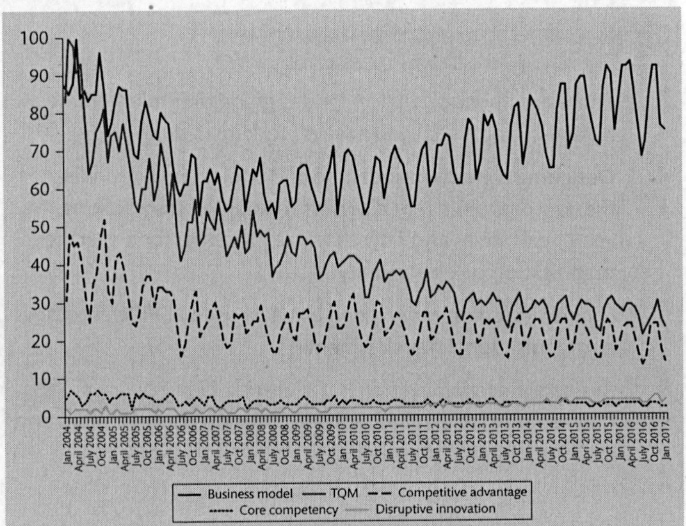

FIGURE 0.1 2004–17 relative Google searches for business models and other terms

Data source: Google Trends (**www.google.com/trends**)

A business model is a rather strange thing.
A great business model is obvious, at least in hindsight.

A free, ad-based website to search the entire internet? Google has a great business model, but the unimaginably large dataset Google has amassed fuels dozens of other business models in both related and unrelated fields.

A terrible business model is often obvious, too. Shipping heavy, bulky pet food directly to consumers? High shipping costs on relatively low margin product turned out to be disastrous for Pets.com. Twenty years later, however, pet food can be purchased with free shipping on Amazon. Clearly, timing makes a difference. Perhaps this whole business model concept is more complex than it looks.

Here is the bottom line on business models:

The bottom line of great business models

- There are *no magic bullets* for designing or implementing a business model that will always work in all situations.
- Designing a great business model requires *understanding the key organisational elements* (resources, transactions, value, narrative) and *how they work together* for a specific organisation or opportunity.
- *Different business model tools* are best used at *different stages* of organisational development.
- *Business model innovation is a high-risk, high-reward process* that requires a balance between focus on competencies and creative opportunity-seeking.

Business models are the heart of your firm's value proposition.

This book shows you how to create, test, adapt and innovate business models. Great business models drive rapid growth; bad business models can doom the most promising ventures.

Perhaps you have read about business models or led a discussion at your firm about business model change. You have wanted to investigate it, but suspect you do not really know your organisation's business model. Perhaps you have avoided the topic because the books and consultants all seem to say different things. This book is different: it provides all the basic information you need, clear and concise examples, and direct advice on how to think about business models at your organisation.

We combine the latest research, straightforward tools and current examples to bring this surprisingly tricky topic to life. Straightforward cases from our research and experience highlight key lessons. This book applies a new life-cycle based approach to make business models relevant to your company's development stage. Your company changes over time – so should your business model.

It does not matter what you think you know about business models. It does not matter if you are a seasoned executive, a mid-level manager, a small business owner, an entrepreneur (or a wannabe), or just someone with an interest in business and management. The popular and scholarly media are filled with hyperbolic, unproven claims about what business models are, how to build them and how they determine success and growth.

Put all of that aside. It is time to set the record straight.

It is time to design, build and adapt business ideas that thrive.

Part 1

The business model

In this section, we explore how the business model came to dominate popular and scholarly conversations about management, especially entrepreneurship. We carefully consider what business models *are* and *are not*. Finally, we explore what we know for sure about business models and how you can use that to build and grow viable organisations. This overview will pave the way for a richer and more practical approach to designing, building and adapting business models for real organisations.

1 Real business models

'I don't have a business model.'

Sal Khan, founder of Khan Academy, which has delivered billions of free education lessons to students around the world

Until the dot-com boom of the late 1990s, no one needed to explain a business model to run a successful organisation. Today, scholars, managers and consultants insist that the business model is the holy grail of organisational survival, scale and profitability.

Have no doubt, the 'business model' can be an important, effective tool in the manager's toolkit. Organisational leaders should know the basic elements of a business model and how those elements work together. A business model provides valuable insight into every organisation, regardless of industry, field, geography or size. Business models are relevant to for-profit and not-for-profit firms alike. Business models can be applied to academic institutions and governments. If there is *organisation,* there is a *business model.*

Why business models work

No one knows.

The simple, unvarnished truth is that the *science* of business models provides no real explanations for how or why some business models work and some fail. We do not have solid research evidence for how entrepreneurs create new business models or a foolproof method for evaluating a business model on paper. A significant amount of rigorous business model research relies on business model definitions that are quite different from how managers think about business models. Even solid scientific findings may not be relevant to entrepreneurs.

The business model is not like most other management concepts. For example, corporate strategy describes how your firm competes against others. As with most management concepts, strategy can be benchmarked against other organisations. If you can make the same product at a lower cost, you may be able to outperform other organisations. That would be a good strategy; implemented effectively, it leads to profits and growth.

A good business model may have no comparison to existing businesses; it might not even be in an existing industry or market!

New business model example: Priceline

What is Priceline? The company has now broadly extended its services, but it is useful to look at the organisation's business model at the very beginning (online in 1998). To the end consumer, it looked like a travel company, but it provided no actual travel services. To the travel industry, it looked like a marketing channel, but there was no formal partnership – Priceline actively hid the names of the travel providers. The business model was brilliant – use the internet to create real-time, blind auctions of extra travel industry capacity such as empty hotel rooms and airline seats. Technically, Priceline was an online auctioneer; at the time, there was no market for 'unbranded' travel.

The business model challenge is deceptively simple. Great business models work because the elements are aligned in support of the value creation process. But even that alignment may not be obvious. Consider Southwest Airlines, the precursor to low-cost air carriers around the world. Nearly everything about Southwest's business model was designed to minimise costs. Southwest flew only one type of plane to optimise maintenance. It flew out of smaller regional airports to minimise gate fees. It kept pricing simple to minimise selling costs. Yet it paid higher than average wages and spent more than other airlines on training and incentive packages. Why? Because in the airline industry small employee errors generate high costs. A late departure could impact multiple routes; if passengers or luggage miss a connection, the airline incurs high costs in customer service. If the firm's profit margin is 10 per cent, then $100 in costs incurred resolving a customer service problem requires $1,000 in additional revenue to make up the loss. Southwest's low-cost business model required a relatively high-cost human resource element. The business model was very effective: for two decades Southwest was consistently more profitable than the rest of the US airline industry. In some years, it was more profitable than the rest of the industry combined.

But Southwest is not the only low-cost carrier model. Ryanair has been extremely successful in Europe with much lower investments in human resources. It uses a dramatically different pricing structure to ensure that planes are full, the single most critical operating rule for airlines. Southwest generally is seen as a great company to work for with great customer service; Ryanair is called out regularly for poor service and has been repeatedly fined by various government authorities for customer service problems. Both 'low-cost carriers' are profitable and growing. In other words, business models are complicated.

Business model do's and don'ts

Do use business model analysis to think about how organisations are designed to create value.

Don't be fooled by the apparent simplicity of high-level descriptions of business models of large organisations. The larger the organisation and the more complex its product/service mix, the more likely that there are multiple business models in play. Large companies that appear to use the same 'business models' may have dramatically different elements working under the surface.

Creating and capturing value

Before we go any further, we need to agree, at least temporarily, on what a business model is. In Chapter 2 we will discuss the history and research on business models, but we need a placeholder to help frame the discussion.

Business models have nearly always been discussed and described in the context of two key organisational concepts. The first is *value creation*. Business models have something to do with how (and why) organisations create value. The second concept is *design*. Business models have something to do with how organisations function, specifically in terms of the structures and relationships that govern behaviours and activities.

In other words, a business model is the organisational design used to exploit an opportunity and create value.

Every organisation exists for a single purpose: to create more value than an individual could do alone. That value could be profit, education, economic growth, social justice, entertainment or any number of other possible outcomes. An organisation uses various forms of capital (human, financial, physical, etc.) to create and capture that value.

Sal Khan originally wanted to provide mathematics instruction, from a distance, to his nephew. He recorded relatively simple videos demonstrating mathematical concepts with a voiceover. Then he made those videos available to his nephew, and anyone else, via the internet. Khan Academy scales that value creation to millions of people globally.

Worksheet 1.1

GETTING A GRIP ON VALUE

Whether you are a business model novice or pro, you need to come to grips with the hard reality of value creation and capture. Go to the 'Worksheets' section of the website for the book. Open or download Worksheet 1.1: Getting a grip on value. Completing the activity should take less than 5 minutes, but you will come back to it throughout the book. All you need to do is clearly and simply explain how your organisation creates and captures value. There is also an example for you to try your hand before the serious business of evaluating your own organisation.

In the specific case of for-profit companies, value created must be *captured* in a familiar form: money. Technically, every good business model captures value. For example, effective non-governmental organisations (NGOs) create change, usually to accomplish a social purpose or agenda. The NGO may use outcome data to fundraise or recruit but, in most cases, the outcome itself does not fuel the organisation's operations. At for-profit companies, the business model should explicitly link value creation and capture, because the financial outputs of the organisation are also an input. The profits fund development and growth and reward the owners.

Business model impact: Khan Academy

Khan Academy has become one of the most influential and controversial educational innovations of the twenty-first century. Teachers and scholars disagree about the effectiveness of independent, distance-based learning without schedules or grades. The raw usage statistics, however, are difficult to ignore. In 2015, the Khan Academy website was visited by more than 15 million unique visitors each month. It offers more than 100,000 different videos and lessons on subjects, ranging from basic addition to quantum mechanics and art history. Those lessons, developed in English, are now available in dozens of other languages. Every lesson and every course is free. Sal Khan may not have had a business model. Khan Academy, however, has leveraged one man's vision for education into a global phenomenon.

Test in the real world

The hard truth is that there is no single, surefire test of a business model other than to try it out in the real world.

The good news is that many business models can be pilot tested. Later in the book we will look at how to transition from a business model design to a real-world test. Unless very large economies of scale or network effects are inherent to value creation or capture, small-scale tests are generally effective for identifying business model bottlenecks and inefficiencies.

The bad news is that business models can be copied. Business models cannot be protected with patents, trademark or copyright. By their nature, business models cannot be hidden as a trade secret. An organisation's business model is, fundamentally, what it does to create value. Customers, suppliers, partners and even competitors are going to have access to some or all of the details. A good business model for one opportunity or organisation may fail for another in the real world. Uber's ride-sharing business model has now been adapted globally by firms such as Grab (Singapore), Hailo (London), Lyft (USA), Ola (India) and Didi (China). But not all of them are identical or successful. Even Uber, which works elsewhere, was not particularly successful in China and had to exit the market.

Business model hazard: replicating FoodUSA.com

Consider FoodUSA.com. Like Priceline and many other dot-com companies, FoodUSA attempted to use the internet to disintermediate a market. In this case, it was the market for meat. Slaughterhouses and processors could post information anonymously about available product on FoodUSA's electronic marketplace and buyers could bid for what they needed. The highly consolidated food industry kept profits relatively low at the slaughterhouses; FoodUSA was designed to shift the balance of power towards the slaughterhouses and the farmers and still take a commission on every sale.

We will never really know if the business model was long-term viable or not. Despite raising millions of dollars of venture capital and facilitating more than $35 million in transactions, FoodUSA was out of business in less than three years. Why? The business model was copied – by a consortium of the food industry companies that purchased meat from the slaughterhouses. Commerce Ventures, LLC was set up specifically to compete with FoodUSA. It was 55 per cent owned by Tyson Foods and 27 per cent by Cargill, two of the world's largest food companies, along with three other meat producing and processing firms. Even though Commerce Ventures never launched operations at scale, the slaughterhouses stopped posting product with FoodUSA. Cash flow stopped, venture capital dried up and FoodUSA was gone. Commerce Ventures did not outcompete FoodUSA, but its presence made the FoodUSA business model too fragile.

A great business model in one industry may not work in another. On the other hand, a dead business model may be resurrected when circumstances change. Industry context, market conditions, and even time, make a difference. For example, there have been several iterations of business models for music sharing online. Napster is gone, but Spotify, iTunes®, SoundCloud and even YouTube have succeeded in different ways, serving different markets, needs and customer segments.

It may be true that no two business models are *exactly* alike. Changes in technological infrastructure can radically rewrite the rules about what business models are viable or even possible. Most underlying business model elements, however, are familiar to most business people. If you have seen 100 business models, the 101st is likely to show some similarities or element patterns to the ones you have already seen. This is why venture capitalists want entrepreneurs to explain a new venture's business model in clear terms, often with visual diagrams. Similarly, start-ups may copy tried and tested models in new markets with adaptations.

In the gaming industry, an ecosystem of businesses supports many similar firms with slight (but important) variations. Major players, such as Sony, Microsoft and Nintendo, develop and publish software to complement their own hardware platforms. But there is also a large ecosystem of players and businesses supporting these players. Supercell, the Finnish mobile game publisher, has major products such as Clash Royale and Clash of Clans, played by 100 million gamers every day. Tencent, a Chinese internet and payments conglomerate, acquired Supercell in 2016 to consolidate their gaming credentials as a global player. If you go further east, you find a variety of platform providers for gamers, such as Garena in Singapore, which targets the Southeast Asian market. Mixi (Japan) started with a mobile game called Monster Strike, but became so popular that it expanded into a social networking site. Gaming is so popular in South Korea that professional gaming is termed officially as e-sport supplied by growing, profitable companies like Netmarble or Gravity. Smaller, niche markets, such as Vietnam, also have reasonably sized gaming companies, such as VNG. Just in this one sector we observe a plurality of business models and businesses that target specific geographic markets and have marginally differentiated capabilities that allow them to flourish. A business model does not have to be unique, but it does have to be differentiated by your firm's resources, transactions and value creation for you to survive and grow.

Video resource

Geoff Yang, founding partner of California's Redpoint Ventures, explains that nearly every business model has been tried somewhere.

The activities and frameworks in this book cannot substitute for real-world testing. They do, however, provide valuable tools for preparing for that real-world testing. They should also provide a troubleshooting guide to fix damaged or broken business models.

Worksheet 1.2

WHAT'S WRONG WITH MY BUSINESS MODEL?

Before you move on to the next chapter and learn about the history of business models, take a look at Worksheet 1.2. Think about what might not be working in your organisation's business model. You might start by thinking about business

> models of other organisations that you believe do not work well either. The activity should take you only a couple of minutes and will help prepare you for the more detailed business model building activities in the rest of the book.

What makes a great business model?

A great business model is the foundation of a viable organisation. A great business model:

- meets a customer need;
- builds value for the firm and the firm's partners;
- leverages and extends valuable capabilities or resources;
- is efficient;
- differentiates the firm; and
- is sustainable beyond the near-term.

Let us briefly discuss each of these.

Every viable and sustainable organisation serves a core purpose: meeting a need. A great business model might solve a market need and generate revenues and profits; it might address a societal need and generate donations and positive social outcomes. In rare cases, it might create an entirely new need. Regardless, every viable business model meets a need that is not being fully addressed. A business model that does not meet a need simply is not viable.

Meeting a need is necessary but not sufficient. A great business model builds value for the firm and the firm's partners. Business models that do not build value for the organisation are still not viable. Business models that build value for the organisation are viable, but may not be sustainable. Some business models simply transfer value from one organisation to another or across parts of the supply chain. If there is no value creation, then the organisation is likely splitting up value amongst more parties. Great business models are sustainable. They create value for both the organisation and its business partners. That generates a synergistic relationship that benefits all the parties.

At the same time, a business model should leverage and extend the organisation's valuable capabilities and resources. In other words, the business model does not deplete a finite set of resources, like raw materials. Instead, it ensures that the longer the organisation operates, the more effective and valuable it becomes to customers and partners. The most valuable resources are the ones that can be improved, not the ones that get used up. For example, the capability to design high-quality cars is more valuable than the steel that is used in the manufacturing process. The steel is used and replaced, but a top-notch designer becomes more experienced and sophisticated over time.

A great business model is efficient. In the long run, a wasteful business model is vulnerable to industry changes and business model innovation.

Great business models clearly differentiate the organisation from competitors and industry participants. It is common to find numerous organisations in one industry using the same business model. Sometimes, this has been referred to as a sort of organisational dominant design or a special case of contingency theory. The general idea is that organisations tend to migrate to a proven way of doing business and any deviation from that template tends to reduce profitability. The fact is, however, that some of the most effective business models have deviated from industry standard. Consider Alibaba in e-commerce, Southwest in airlines, Apple in computers, Tesla in automotive and Tencent in payments, and so on. At the least, a strong business model ensures that the organisation does not merely replicate what every other firm is doing.

All of these add up to long-term sustainability. The real goal of a great business model is to provide the organisation with the potential to survive and thrive. The best organisations use that success to adapt or innovate the business model to stay ahead of the rest of the industry.

RECAP

- Business models are all about organisational design and value creation.
- An effective business model leverages organisation to scale value creation.
- Business model elements may be aligned in counter-intuitive ways.
- Business models are usually more complicated than they look.
- A good business model in one industry may not work in another.

2 A brief history

The 'business model' as a management concept is still relatively new. Yet it now dominates numerous management conversations. It has become the primary tool for exploring start-ups, entrepreneurship, innovation and key areas of corporate strategy, such as organisational renewal. In this chapter, we will take a brief walk down memory lane to see how the conversation about business models got started.

'Before the late 1990s, no one was using the phrase "business model". Or at least, it hardly appeared in written form. The phrase has since morphed, subtly but quickly, from an abstract theoretical term to one with animate, even living connotations.'

Anna Codrea-Rado, writing for QZ.com, April 17 2013

If you are in a hurry to build or change business models, this is probably the one chapter you could skip for now. At the same time, understanding this history helps explain why managers and scholars talk about business models in certain ways. It also highlights some of the limitations of business models. If you choose to skip ahead, come back to this chapter when you have time, because you will get useful guidance and thoughtful perspective on what business models really are.

Models of business

The origins of the 'business model' go back only about 50 years. In the 1960s, management scholars were attempting to deconstruct every aspect of business operations. This effort was driven by a number of important scholarly questions about management and strategy. Questions such as:

- 'How do managers make decisions without full information?'
- 'Why do companies in the same industry look similar, yet not exactly the same?'
- 'Why do some companies consistently outperform others?'
- 'Why does change help some companies but hurt or destroy others?'

Some academics began exploring whether they could create 'models of business'. These were efforts to use software to simulate all of the activities of an organisation. The primary intent was to explain management decisions within a completely rational framework. These efforts generated fascinating insights into some decision processes, such as pricing. But they never developed into a science of 'business models'.

By the 1970s, scholarship in management science had changed dramatically. Decision making and business outcomes research had refocused on frameworks of cognition, strategy, organisational behaviour and social psychology. Mentions of business models in the academic literature before the late 1990s are few and far between. The same is true for publications targeting business professionals. For example, the phrase 'business model' is mentioned in only six articles in *Harvard Business Review* in the entire decade of the 1970s, and in only eleven articles in the 1980s. Until the late 1990s, the business model concept was, for all intents and purposes, dormant. If you are interested in business models as 'models of business', check out the Models of Business Excursion on the BMB website for more information, including a mention in a Nobel Prize acceptance speech.

Simple business models

In the 1990s, something happened to the way scholars and business people thought about companies and innovation. It would be easy, but misleading, to link this change entirely to the nascent development of the internet. The idea of a 'business model' as a holistic description of how a firm creates value had been percolating under the surface of discussions about strategy and competitive advantage. The phrase was coming into common use in the managerial world.

Early uses of the business model concept were usually simplified analogies for how a firm creates value. One of the most famous examples is the 'razor and razor blade' sales model. This is used to describe how some firms sell cheaply or even give away one product (the razor handle) in order to generate long-term demand for a complementary product that must be purchased regularly and repeatedly (the disposable razor blade).

Managers and scholars were beginning to use business models as a shorthand for the unique ways that firms created value. In an HBR 'perspectives' discussion from 1993, Bob Lurie, one of the founders of Monitor Company, identified the challenge of distinguishing good strategic ideas from good execution. He stated: 'IKEA has performed well with a *not-terribly-original business model* that, in less skilful hands, may well have failed.'

By the end of the decade, the business model had taken hold in the world of management practice. Business models had become a buzzword. Accenture's Institute for Strategic Change (formerly Andersen Consulting) published a guide that tried to identify every *possible* business model. It includes the 'razor and blade' model, along with 33 others, divided neatly into categories such as 'price models' and 'innovation models'. The report also suggests a variant of 'change models' that provides one of the first dynamic approaches to business models.

Worksheet 2.1

DOES MY ORGANISATION HAVE A STANDARD BUSINESS MODEL?

There will probably never be a list of all possible complete list of business models. It is helpful, however, to think about whether your business model fits reasonably well into a specific category. This is an opportunity to see if your business model fits into a relatively well-defined category and can be explained with a relatively simple analogy. Another possibility is that your business model is a combination of categories, or perhaps something totally new and different.

E-business model confusion

In the late 1990s, an amazing technological, cultural and social phenomenon unfolded. The development and deployment of the internet, primarily via the infrastructure of the world wide web, has had an unparalleled impact on society and business.

It would also totally muck up the study and practice of business models.

The 'business model' was, as academics might say, a 'term of art'. It entered the language of management practice referring to firm-level value creation whilst, at the same time, taking into account certain high-level operational patterns. But it clearly meant different things in different contexts to different people. The advent of the internet, and so-called 'e-businesses', would turn the nascent conversation about business models into a Tower of Babel.

The concept of an 'e-business model' was a framework for internet-based businesses similar to the 'models of business' framework from the 1960s. The key difference was that these models were focused primarily on transactions, precisely because the internet facilitated transactions at a fraction of the normal cost. Money, information and goods could be exchanged with significantly less human involvement.

The focus of these models was, of course, new ventures or new business units that operated primarily or entirely via web-based or other electronic interfaces. Specific transactions could be clearly delineated, broken into subcomponents and rebuilt in other ways. Managers and scholars generated sets of transactions organised and categorised into a limited set of 'atomic' e-business models. These included, for example, content providers, direct-to-customer and value net integrators.

The problem, of course, was distinguishing between an 'e-business model' and a 'business model' for an organisation that operates with some or all of its activities enabled by the internet. The world of 'e-business models' has become a relatively specialised topic, generally applied when large organisations with significant physical infrastructure move towards internet-enabled activities and operations. We will not be discussing e-business models further in this book; readers with a specific interest in this topic are directed to Weill and Vitale's *Place to Space: Migrating to eBusiness Models.*

Another source of confusion centred on whether internet-based companies could be valued the same way as 'traditional' firms. Check out the New Business Model Value Excursion on the website for some additional information on this topic, including an ill-fated prediction by an eminent management professor about this 'new value creation', just months before the dot-com crash.

The lessons of the dot-com boom and bust are very clear:

- Do explore business models that create value for customers in new ways.
- Do not convince yourself that an innovative business model is exempt from traditional measures of value creation. Novelty might distract from output metrics for a while, but not forever. The best business models generate real, measurable results.

Business models in theory and practice

The dot-com bubble burst, but the business model emerged even stronger. Business models were not unique to dot-com companies; every viable organisation has a business model with demonstrable value creation. A clear definition, however, remained elusive. What exactly is a business model? Is there a finite set of business models? Can business models be grouped into types? Do some business models perform better than others? Why?

Arguably the most important scholarly research on business models has been conducted by Professor Raphael Amit and

Professor Christoph Zott. In 2001, they published the first research article about business models in a top management journal. They asked a seemingly simple question: Why do e-businesses seem to create more value than other businesses? Their answer: new business models. In particular, they clarified that the business model was a new way to think about how companies create value and provided the first, and arguably most, logically consistent definition for a business model.

In their paper 'Value Creation in E-business', Amit and Zott paved the way for research on the business model as an important new concept. They stated:

'Our findings suggest that no single entrepreneurship or strategic management theory can fully explain the value creation potential of e-business. Rather, an integration of the received theoretical perspectives on value creation is needed. To enable such an integration, we offer the business model construct as a unit of analysis for future research on value creation in e-business. A business model depicts the design of transaction content, structure, and governance so as to create value through the exploitation of business opportunities.'

You do not have to agree with this definition to use business models, but it might be worth a bit more thought. Amit and Zott argued that a business model is the *design of the transactions a firm uses to create value.* This includes internal and external transactions – everything, in effect, the firm does where information or assets are exchanged. This is a very powerful definition, because it is very precise and yet very comprehensive. No subsequent explanation for the business model (including the authors' contributions) are quite as elegant.

There were, however, two downsides to their work. First, the definition is non-obvious and somewhat difficult to incorporate into simple, practical management tools. Second, the key study by Amit and Zott utilised data from the dot-com boom, and a significant amount of the 'value creation' they reference did not survive the dot-com bubble. For example, they profiled three companies with extraordinary value creation: Autobytel, Cyberian Outpost and Ricardo.de. The combined value of these firms dropped by at least 80 per cent when the dot-com bubble burst. Having an 'innovative' business model was not enough to guarantee long-term value creation.

Since that article, hundreds of scholars have written thousands of peer-reviewed research papers about business models. Searching 'business model' in Google Scholar generates more than half a million results; limiting it to 'business model' in the title still generates more than 12,000 results. To date, no clear consensus has emerged on exactly what a business model is or precisely how to study or measure it in a rigorous way. See Excursion 5 for more information, including a sampling of business model definitions used by academic researchers.

Our own research showed the other side of the problem. Scholars studying business models rarely incorporated either direct information or observations from managers about how business models were actually being used in the real world. How useful are research results in the field of management if they do not reflect how managers think or what they do? Bad enough that management scholars could not agree with each other, but they clearly did not agree with managers! Extensive interviews and surveys of managers showed that the variety of business model definitions proposed and tested by scholars simply did not reflect how managers thought about business models.

As good as the Amit and Zott definition is, it does not match how entrepreneurs and managers think about business models. Faced with a choice between a more rigorous academic definition and something that managers can use, we have chosen the latter.

Managers think about business models as the convergence of three critical organisational elements: resources, transactions and value creation. To managers, *business models link the design of the organisation to the opportunity the organisation creates or solves.*

The Business Model Canvas arrives

The most important advance in business model *practice* arrived with Alexander Osterwalder's Business Model Canvas in his book *Business Model Generation.* The first part of the original book is available as a free download.

The Business Model Canvas is a practical management tool for thinking about business models. Based on discussions with hundreds of managers, entrepreneurs and scholars, Osterwalder developed a relatively straightforward set of business model elements and an aesthetically pleasing design for mapping them. The canvas identified nine business model elements: key resources, key activities, key partners, value propositions, customer relationships, channels, customer segments, revenues and costs.

The canvas was an important step forward for three reasons. First, it provided a reasonable and useful balance of the key ideas developed by scholars. Second, it offered an effective visual mechanism for organising thinking and discussion about a specific business model. Finally, it emphasised that a critical issue for designing, evaluating and changing business models is how the elements fit together, not just what the elements are. We will look at the Business Model Canvas in more depth in Chapter 7.

The future of the business model

How active is research on business models? In a word: very!

Figure 2.1 shows how rapidly research publications are increasing, especially in contrast with other key management topics.

Like all business buzzwords, the 'business model' has evolved from something new and exciting to something more mundane and straightforward. New buzzwords will emerge. The business model will be one more framework taught in business schools, used by consultants and analysed by venture capitalists.

The success of the Business Model Canvas has led to similar tools, such as the Lean Canvas, the Business Model Zen Canvas and others. Any of these can provide a valuable process for evaluating an entrepreneurial opportunity.

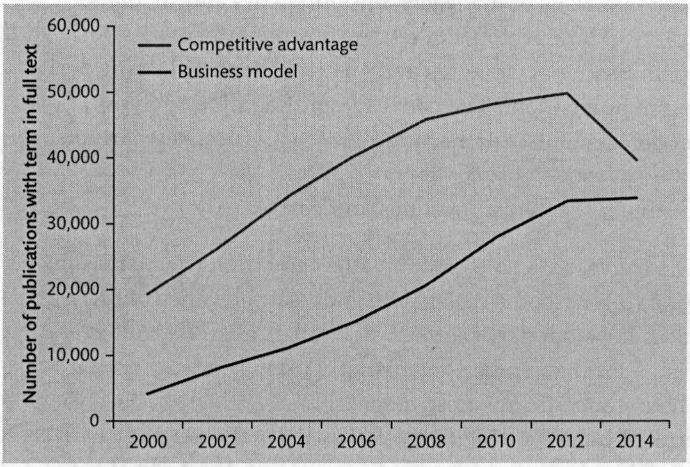

FIGURE 2.1 Number of scholarly publications published with 'business model' and 'competitive advantage' in full text

Source: Google Scholar

The value of a business model tool is not embedded in the tool itself. Using the tool does not guarantee success! The benefit of a business model tool comes from the structured process of clarifying assumptions, thinking about how organisational elements work together.

In the coming years, academic scholars will publish more research on business models. All of it will probably be useful, in the sense that it will further knowledge about how organisations explore and exploit opportunities. On the other hand, most of it likely will be disconnected from practice in which entrepreneurs and managers make difficult decisions about new ideas with limited time and resources. In addition, research on business models is often so narrowly focused that the findings are either irrelevant to most organisations or effectively impossible to use. Further, the rapid pace of technological change in some fields, such as information technology, combined with the relatively lengthy timeframes required to publish management research, means that academic research on business models is often out of date when it is published. As academics, we are hopeful that business model research will become more substantive and cumulative over time.

You might be asking, 'What does all this mean for me?'

Business models are an important tool when launching a new venture or building a growth company. Business model analysis provides a simple and effective framework for evaluating new opportunities. Exploring a venture's business model helps identify key questions and low-cost experiments to test the validity of the opportunity.

If you manage a family or lifestyle business, business models are still very relevant. In many cases, the managers of family and lifestyle businesses have never had to think explicitly about the organisation's business model. Managers at these firms can benefit significantly from business model analysis because it will help explore the underlying assumptions that led to the firm's formation and original success. Most firms cannot remain static forever; exploiting new opportunities requires change.

If you are a senior manager at a large company, non-profit foundation, educational institution or other non-commercial organisation, then you still can benefit from business models. Every organisation has a business model. Business models can be constructed, tested and evaluated. The business model is a key indicator of whether or not the organisation is viable. Managers at these types of organisations generally do not think about business models, which means that the analysis is likely to generate unexpected and eye-opening results.

New business models will emerge in time. Innovative business models tend to follow significant changes in large-scale infrastructure. Changes in technological, social and legal frameworks create new value creation opportunities. Accessing those new sources of value often will require entirely new business model structures.

RECAP

- Managers and scholars have not always thought about 'business models' in the same way.
- The business model is one of the newest tools in the management toolkit.
- New and innovative business models still have to create measurable value.
- If there is organisation, there is a business model!

3 No shortcuts

'The reason why it is so difficult for existing firms to capitalize on disruptive innovations is that [the processes and business model] that make them good at the existing business actually make them bad at competing for the disruption.'

Clayton Christensen

Business models hold endless promise.

Entrepreneurs use new business models to bring innovations to market. Venture capitalists know that a viable business model facilitates rapid growth. CEOs need business models at large firms to adapt to technological and socio-demographic change. Smart policymakers recognise that business models underlie long-term economic development, job growth and even effective provisioning of government services.

The good news is that a business model is a nearly universal construct. It can be applied, with varying degrees of specificity and effectiveness, to new ventures, family businesses, growing companies, multinational corporations, industries, governments and possibly even nations. Business models identify the key elements and structures of an organisation. Business model analysis reveals how an organisation can improve to meet market needs and create value, whether that value is measured in profit or less tangible human good.

The bad news is that there are no one-step magic bullets for creating, evaluating, adapting or implementing business models, brilliant or otherwise. There are many tools and frameworks to aid the process, but their simplicity is deceptive. Designing, testing and launching great business models requires an investment in knowledge, expertise and informed intuition. Without that investment, entrepreneurs may run afoul of many obstacles.

The obstacles to designing great business models

There are numerous obstacles to great business models. First, the path of least resistance in generating business models will be to rely on what you already know. Second, the critical, granular information that you need to generate or assess truly innovative business models may be non-obvious or difficult to access. Third, communicating business model innovation and change can be very difficult. Fourth, it is easy to focus on the wrong level of detail when thinking about business models. Finally, the critical element for evaluation and testing, business model coherence, is usually neither simple nor obvious. We will explore these in detail and use some examples to see the challenge. At each stage, it would be a good idea to complete the activity to track your assumptions about the business model at your organisation.

What you already know is the path of least resistance

In business, you know what you know. Generally, you do not know what you do not know. It is hard to be aware of your own knowledge gaps. With business models, this is especially problematic, because the business model is a shorthand for how an organisation creates value. Business models are often conveyed as simple explanations or stories. Those stories will make intuitive sense to people at the organisation as well as outside stakeholders. It is an extremely efficient way to convey a significant amount of information about the organisation. Because it is so efficient and convincing, it tends to override contrary data or alternative options.

We regularly ask university students and entrepreneurs to map out the business model for a specific venture or organisation. In most cases, they can provide a surprisingly clear and insightful map or canvas in 10–15 minutes. We then ask them to change the business model or build an alternative business model to compete with alternate products for different customers. The vast majority either get completely stuck or unintentionally generate the same business model map. Even if we supply them with alternative data about a specific market segment, customer need or channel mechanism, there is a natural tendency to revert to what is already in place. 'If it ain't broke, don't fix it.'

High-impact business model analysis requires abandoning core assumptions about how your organisation currently creates value. You might, ultimately, return to your current business model as the best option. But you cannot be certain if you rely on the assumptions that underlie the business model that is currently in use.

Worksheet 3.1

ASSUMPTIONS AND COUNTER-ASSUMPTIONS

Go the website and download Worksheet 3.1. You will be using this to think about ways to overcome the five obstacles to great business models. You should start by writing down three or four key assumptions at the foundation of your organisation's current business model. Do not worry if this seems difficult – everyone struggles with this first time around. It is worth your time to put some ideas on paper, even if they are only partially formed. Then try to create counter-assumptions. You may find that it is easier to find data to test counter-assumptions.

The information you need may be non-obvious or difficult to access

There are no online repositories for data about business models.

High-level estimates for market size and industry profitability may often be found with a single Google search. Researching a business model, on the other hand, often requires extrapolating from limited or tangentially related data.

Identifying and exploring business models usually requires triangulating high-level information with detailed primary research, in-depth brainstorming and company-specific analysis. In cases where business model elements are new or innovative, there simply may not be comparable examples or related data.

Students on one of our courses wanted to evaluate a 'buy one, give one' business model to provide feminine hygiene products to young women in Zimbabwe. Young women in many African countries often miss school because of the stigma associated with menstruation. Assessing this novel and complex business model required data the students simply could not obtain. You can read about this unusual example in the Taurai Foundation Excursion on the BMB website.

> **Worksheet 3.2**
> **WHAT DATA DO YOU NEED?**
>
> Download Worksheet 3.2. Consider the assumptions and counter-assumptions you generated in Worksheet 3.1. What data do you need to test these? How will you get that data?

Communicating business models with analogies can be deceptive

Business models are powerful, in part, because we can use them to generate feedback and sometimes pilot-test opportunities. When business models incorporate complex or unfamiliar elements, however, they may be difficult to communicate clearly and effectively. Unfortunately, the most common 'solution' to this challenge is to generate analogies to familiar innovations.

Mini case: Grappl and the danger of business model analogy

One of our students learned that a great analogy can mask a critical problem. Vash Marada investigated and pilot-tested Grappl, a 'university-specific mobile-based on-demand peer-to-peer tutoring service'. Not quite sure what that is? What if we call it 'Uber for college student tutoring?' Suddenly, it seems a bit more obvious. University students would log in and request a tutor on a specific topic and registered tutors could respond to provide assistance that same day.

In the case of Grappl, the analogy emphasises the power of a just-in-time system. Tutoring, like transportation, is often very time-specific: you need to get somewhere at a specific time or you need to learn a course topic to complete an assignment or prepare for an exam. But the analogy glosses over other significant differences. Consider, for example, the issues of quality and geography. Most drivers have roughly the same competence level and are likely to get you, in one piece, where you need to go. Quality of tutoring varies more dramatically, yet there are no regulations limiting who can tutor. Every Uber driver should have a driver's licence; aside from prior user ratings, there would be no obvious qualifications for university tutors on Grappl. Similarly, the Uber service is pretty much the same in any city; a customer or driver can use it in any city. Grappl tutors can, generally, tutor only on topics that are specific to one university and a limited set of courses.

Once the app was in use, Vash quickly recognised the limits to scaling the business model. He has moved on to more exciting projects, but he does not regret the experience of seeing a business model reach its limits.

Some caution clearly is required when making business model analogies. First, the analogy is rarely perfect. In most cases, the analogy will highlight the elements of the business model that would fit whilst unintentionally hiding elements that do not fit. Second, the analogy explicitly plays on the subjective and emotional value of the comparator. This encourages people to believe they would have recognised the future success of the comparator and they should feel good about recognising the new opportunity. Everyone likes to think they can spot a winner.

Be very cautious about believing, much less creating and using these types of business model analogies.

It is easy to focus on the wrong level of detail

Creating new business models, or changing your current business model, inevitably draws attention to some organisational elements and away from others. Very often, entrepreneurs and managers will tend to focus on the most familiar or verified details.

Maps and canvases are effective tools for generating and evaluating business models. We will use maps and canvases in Part 3 to design and adapt business models. But it is easy to focus on overly simple high-level elements or unnecessarily detailed elements. The mapping and canvassing tools, whilst powerful, may unintentionally prevent you from carefully considering how business model elements interact and function in a real-world organisational context.

The most common error we see is generating a business model canvas with general, high-level elements. This can be a good starting point for getting a basic sense of a business model. In most cases, however, over-generalising business model elements will lead to at least three problems. First, it will not be clear what data needs to be collected to evaluate and test the business model. Second, the elements of the business model will *appear* to work effectively together, simply because there is not enough specificity to generate conflicts. Finally, in the case of business model change or innovation, it will not be realistic to test against the existing organisation.

Less common, but equally problematic, are business model maps that drill down to extremely granular details. These maps are often quite convincing, because they seem to present every possible nuance of the business model. In reality, over-specification of business model detail just creates a different set of problems. First, it will often be difficult to assess how business model elements interact because the detailed descriptions appear unrelated. Second, the details may facilitate data collection but simultaneously hide larger problems or missing assumptions. Finally, over-specified business model details tend to come from familiar or existing organisational elements. These may turn out to be correct, but prevent careful investigation of less familiar alternatives.

Worksheet 3.3

THE DEVIL IS IN THE DETAIL

Download Worksheet 3.3. Start by taking a look at the three sample canvases associated with an 'e-parking' business model to address limited parking facilities at a university campus. Weblinks (URLs) are provided on the worksheet for all three canvases). It should be fairly obvious which is underspecified, which is over-specified and which provides about the right level of detail. To complete the activity, download Worksheet 3.4. Then select one business model component (e.g. 'resources', 'channels', etc.) and compare across the canvases. Imagine what data you would collect, given what is provided in each canvas. How would you explain that section of the canvas to a potential employee? A potential investor? Could you improve the section further with additional information?

Business models are complex systems

A business model is a system of elements and connections. Some elements and connections are more important than others. The success of the business model, however, depends on whether the system works effectively as a whole. This is something we will talk about extensively once we begin building business models. You can also read more about it in the Business Model as Coherent System Excursion on the website.

What business models are not

'When I think about business models, I'm reminded of US Supreme Court Justice Potter Stewart addressing the question of pornography: "I shall not today attempt further to define [pornography] . . . and perhaps I could never succeed in intelligibly doing so. But I know it when I see it." As for me, I'm not sure I could define a business model, but I know a business model when I see one'.

John Biondi, serial entrepreneur and director of the 'Discovery to Product' Programme at The University of Wisconsin-Madison (personal interview)

Business models have been mistaken for many other business concepts. Before we consider what really is known about business models, and before we dive into building business models, we should be clear about what business models are *not*.

A business model is not a picture

The tools for evaluating business models are effective and efficient guides for capturing, evaluating, designing and/or changing a firm's business model.

Generating a business model map or canvas provides a valuable representation of organisational elements and, hopefully, how those elements interact to generate value.

The map can be an extremely effective communication tool, allowing managers to convey complex ideas and structures quickly and simply. As noted, however, this simplification often relies on analogies, which may be misleading.

The 'real' business model of an organisation is, ultimately, realised only in the operational combination of resources and activities (transactions) as the firm functions. Generating a business model picture, map or canvas guarantees nothing about how, if or when the business model actually happens. Ultimately, the business model map, picture or canvas is only as useful as its implementation at the organisation.

A business model is not a marketing strategy

'Free-to-play isn't a business model. Free-to-play is a marketing strategy. It's a way to get people over the hump of trying out your game. It gets rid of the friction that happens when you charge an upfront fee.'

Mitch Lasky, Benchmark Capital, Disney, Activision, EA

A common practical misuse of business model analysis is to better explain its value proposition to potential customers. Whilst this is, potentially, an admirable and valuable activity, it is not really business model analysis at all.

Some entrepreneurs, managers and organisations approach business model change or innovation as a potential cure for a perceived mismatch between current organisational capabilities and the needs of the market segment. In theory, business model analysis and (re)design could, in fact, help determine how the firm's products and services could be better marketed. Business model analysis, however, is not primarily intended to resolve marketing issues. In fact, when business model thinking is shrewdly applied to marketing problems, it often generates unexpected or even unwanted results. Managers looking for a quick fix for a perceived weakness in marketing are sometimes presented with a radical process redesign of customer relationship management, or an entirely new value creation process to address unmet customer needs. These could well be useful or necessary, but they could also simply mask poor marketing implementation.

A business model is not an investor pitch

Venture capitalists and other private investors were some of the first to appreciate the power of business model analysis. Unlike a business plan, which describes a commercialisation strategy, a business model maps the unique elements of value creation. That can be quite compelling for an investor trying to assess whether or not a new venture has real long-term potential.

Video resource

Ann Miura-Ko of Floodgate Ventures in California explains why venture capitalists want to understand a start-up's business model.

But investors need to see a lot more than just a business model canvas. In fact, it is highly uncommon to see a business model canvas included in an investor pitch. Business model canvases tend to be:

- information-dense and difficult to display in an actual presentation or written report;
- filled with shorthand, company-specific jargon or acronyms that are not obvious to an outside observer; and
- unlikely to convey the most critical success factors or unique innovations because everything in the canvas appears to be of the same level of importance.

A business model is not a demonstration or test of profitability

A business model analysis can clarify whether the pieces of an organisation can be combined and coordinated to create value. In theory, good business model analysis helps identify whether or not an organisation, such as a for-profit business, is viable or not.

A business model does not directly demonstrate or test whether or not a business will be profitable. Business model analysis can help point the way towards organisational components and structures aligned with corporate strategy. Profitability results primarily from strategic implementation in a competitive context. A business model can be a powerful input to your overall strategic plan, but it will not replace your strategic plan or deployment.

A business model is not an opportunity evaluation

A business model can explain how an organisation could exploit an opportunity. But the business model does not address whether the underlying opportunity is inherently attractive or not. One of the hard lessons of entrepreneurship is that not all opportunities are created equal. Some opportunities are bigger, some are easier to access and some have more long-term potential.

Assessing opportunity attractiveness requires thinking carefully about the target market and the industry context in which the organisation will compete. A thoughtful approach to business model analysis can help explore this. But the business model framework provides no specific evaluation of how attractive an opportunity is.

An excellent resource on evaluating opportunities is *The New Business Road Test* by John Mullins, published by Pearson Financial Times. We use *The New Business Road*

Test as a compact (and inexpensive) textbook for many of our entrepreneurship courses. Newer editions of the book include an introductory discussion about business models and Lean start-up methodology. Mullins argues that you should conduct the 'Road Test' before you write a detailed business plan. We agree completely! Further, we think you should follow up the 'Road Test' with business model analysis before you write the business plan. A business plan without a business model is just speculation.

A business model is not a corporate strategy

Managers and scholars have struggled to clarify the relationship between business models and corporate strategy. Some scholarly publications that would otherwise appear to address 'strategic' issues claim to study business models. For example, airlines such as Southwest and Ryanair have long been identified as a clear case of implementing a low-cost strategy. In recent years, however, business researchers have begun referring to these as examples of 'low-cost carrier business models'.

Corporate strategy (or competitive strategy) is one of the oldest, most important and well-developed of all management topics in research and practice. Does a business model subsume corporate strategy? Or perhaps a business model is just a component of a firm's competitive strategy? After all, corporate strategy deals with resources, transactions and competitive advantage and value creation. Are business models and strategy just the same, in the end?

They are not the same. Strategy addresses positioning against competitors whilst business models are for exploiting new opportunities. But it is easy to confuse them. If you would like to read more about the difference between business models and corporate/competitive strategy, please check out the Business Models and Strategy Excursion on the website.

RECAP

In this chapter we discussed why there are no magic bullets to great business models:

- There are numerous obstacles to effective business model analysis.
- Business models are easily misunderstood as a variety of other organisational elements and concepts.
- Business model analysis is a learned skill that requires knowledge and practice.

4 What we know for sure

'It's the business model, stupid!'

Esther Dyson

The biggest problem with business models is that we do not really know why some business models work whilst others fail. To date, the scholarly research on business models has not produced clear methods for measuring business model components, processes or outcomes.

For example, there is no evidence that entrepreneurs that use a business model canvas are more likely to successfully launch a venture than those who do not use a canvas. There is no research that clearly demonstrates the requirements for a 'new' or 'innovative' business model.

Some research studies suggest that innovative business models are more profitable than extant business models, but there has been no consistency in business model variables across these studies. In many studies, the definition of the 'business model' or 'business model innovation' is left primarily to the interpretation of the managers participating in interviews or filling out surveys. One of the ironies of research on business models is that whilst academics struggle to find a consistent and clear definition, managers tend to assume that everyone has roughly the same understanding of what a business model is.

So, what do we really know about business models? Given the amount of confusing and sometimes contradictory information about business models and business model innovation, it helps to emphasise what scholars and practitioners have been able to clearly demonstrate. We can summarise what we really know about business models into 10 simple statements:

1. The business model is here to stay.
2. Business models are not clearly tied to performance.
3. Innovative business models can win big.
4. Innovative business models are high risk.
5. Business models do not function in isolation.
6. A business model is only as good as its implementation.
7. Business models change.
8. Business model change is not easy.
9. Organisations can test and implement multiple business models.
10. New business models are impossible to predict in advance.

The business model is here to stay

Buzzword or not, the business model is here to stay for the foreseeable future. It is standard nomenclature in venturing communities around the world. It is well accepted within the broader corporate environment. If you have not already done so, the odds are good that you will talk about business models.

Business models are not clearly tied to performance

Unlike many tools for strategic management, finance, marketing and other business disciplines, business model tools have not been clearly tied to improved performance or even venture survival. Just using a business model framework, such as a canvas, does not guarantee organisational success. If you only take away one lesson from this book, then this is probably the one.

Using a business model framework does not guarantee you will find a viable business model. It does not guarantee you will implement it and build a successful business.

Innovative business models can win big

There probably is a link between truly innovative business models and entrepreneurial success. Companies with innovative business models are often experimenting with novel resources, transaction types or value creation systems. Any of these can facilitate a competitive advantage that leads to success and growth.

India's Bharti Airtel is generally considered one of the great business model innovation success stories in recent history. The company initiated a low infrastructure business model in the mobile phone industry in India. Bharti outsourced nearly every aspect of network infrastructure, challenging the standard operating model used worldwide. By co-opting rural retailers into the sales and distribution systems, Bharti Airtel has grown to the world's fourth largest mobile provider by customer volume.

IBM's survey of more than 700 global CEOs revealed that business model innovation was the most important difference between outperforming and underperforming firms (Figure 4.1).

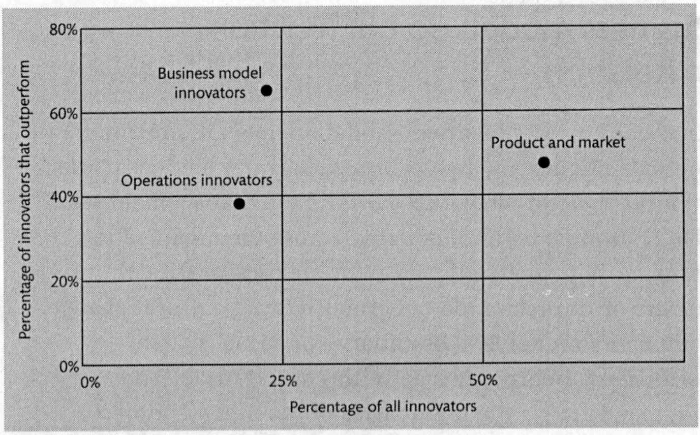

FIGURE 4.1 Performance by innovation type

Source: Based on data from 'Giesen, E., Berman, S.J., Bell, R. and Blitz, A. (2007) 'Three ways to successfully innovate your business model', *Strategy & Leadership*, 35(6), 27–33

Innovative business models are high risk

Business model innovation may generate high rewards, but it is also high risk. Truly innovative business models can just as easily be a recipe for disaster. Consider the business model innovations of Napster and Apple in digital music. Apple's innovation was straightforward – contract with the major music studios to sell songs via a centralised online platform – iTunes®. Napster's innovation was much more dramatic – create a peer-to-peer platform to facilitate exchange of songs by anyone with anyone else. Apple's innovation was primarily transactive, updating the sales and distribution channel to take advantage of low-cost distribution on the internet. Napster's innovation changed all three major business model structures: resources, transactions and value creation. Napster's innovation was so radical that implementing it violated copyright law, which led to Napster being sued and, ultimately, shut down. This is a key lesson: business model innovation can be *too* disruptive.

Business models do not function in isolation

An organisation's business model operates in multiple contexts. Figure 4.2 shows this visually. A business model requires the complete buy-in of the top management team (TMT). It must be implemented across the organisation and simultaneously aligned with the organisational culture or implemented congruently with cultural change. A business model is a 'boundary-spanning' system – it necessarily incorporates activities and transactions that reach across the boundaries of the organisation to suppliers, partners and customers. The business model therefore operates within the context of the firm's supply chain and must contribute to how that supply chain generates value. Finally, the firm's business model is only

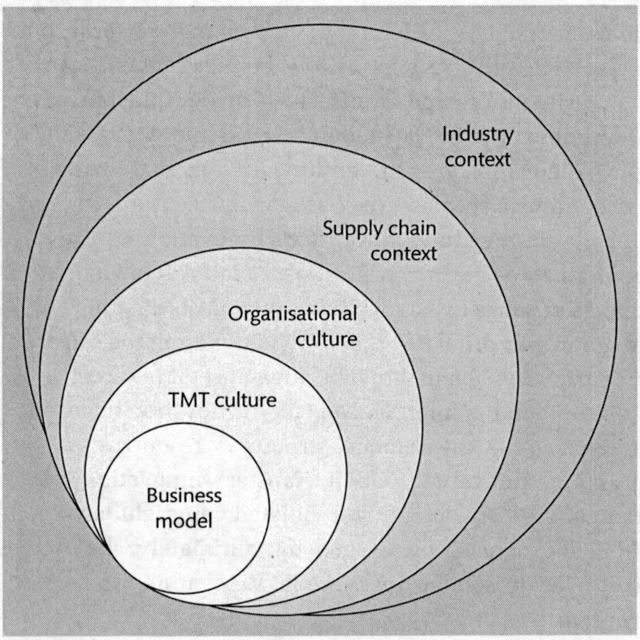

FIGURE 4.2 The business model in context

one business model within a broader industry context. Some industries can support multiple business models and some cannot.

This also emphasises the challenge of business model innovation. Radical changes in a firm's business model have a ripple effect far beyond the benefits and costs to the organisation. Resistance or backlash to change may come from multiple levels.

A business model is only as good as its implementation

A business model is not a picture or a demonstration of profitability. A great business model requires implementation. The entrepreneur or manager must translate the picture or map into a series of processes and activities that utilise and transform organisational resources. A poor or ineffective implementation of a good business model is probably no better than a bad business model. This is why venture investors place so much emphasis on the capabilities of a team. Great implementation can make up for a mediocre business model or adapt the business model on the fly. Poor implementation usually will fail, no matter how good the underlying business model.

Consider the case of Leap Transit. In 2013, a group of entrepreneurs in San Francisco pilot-tested Leap Transit, a private transport system targeting the increasing population of young, well-to-do technology employees in the Bay Area. The business model applied a differentiated model of 'public' transportation, with higher fares, to appeal to a specific niche market that preferred not to commute by car. The innovation seems to make sense, especially for a high-density, high-wealth metropolitan area. Leap raised more than $2.5 million from experienced, professional venture investors and launched services in 2013. But the business model was not implemented effectively. Transportation is a highly regulated industry; the company struggled to obtain a permit for its services from the state of California. Vehicles were not compliant with laws requiring disability accommodations. It was immediately shut down by the government and remained closed through 2014. It relaunched in 2015, but struggled to maintain consistent routes or generate a strong customer base. The state of California again shut the firm down for operating without appropriate licences. Leap Transit filed for bankruptcy before the end of the year.

Business models change

Business model change can be driven by a variety of forces or needs. We will discuss these in detail in Part 4, but a few items are worth noting. Business model adaptation can be driven by management problem solving as a result of *external change*. For example, entrepreneurs or managers may realise that key resources, transactions or value creation no longer effectively connect the company's resources to its market. Alternatively, change may be driven by *internal factors* such as a change of managerial vision or entrepreneurial goals. Research by IBM (Figure 4.3) showed that business model innovation is most commonly driven by four needs: cost reduction, strategic flexibility, specialisation and new market exploitation.

Business model change is not easy

Changing a business model could well be the most difficult change process in all of organisational management.

Why?

Changing an organisation's business model generally requires fundamentally changing how the organisation operates, who it interacts with and how it creates value – possibly all three!

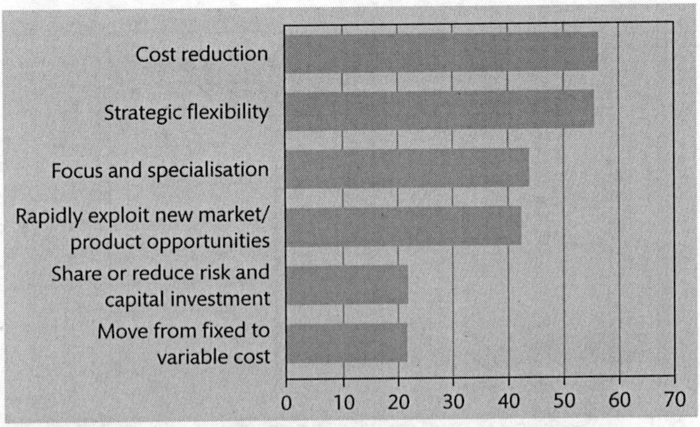

FIGURE 4.3 The most common drivers of business model innovation

Source: Based on data from 'Expanding the innovation horizon: the global CEO study 2006', IBM Global Business Services, March 2006

It is almost inevitable that key people and groups will have to learn unfamiliar skills, acquire unfamiliar resources and develop unfamiliar capabilities.

Unlike strategic change, product innovation or process re-engineering, business model change almost always requires entering unknown territory. The organisation will take on challenges without knowing for certain whether it has the capability to meet those challenges.

Of course, some business model changes are more significant and difficult than others. Broadly speaking, the level of difficulty of business model change is directly related to which, and how many, business model structures need to be changed. It is most difficult to change the value structure; least difficult to change the resource structure. Of course, some business model change requires updating or adapting multiple structures. This increases the challenge, as shown in Figure 4.4.

Some lessons about business model change and innovation are less obvious. For example, our own research showed

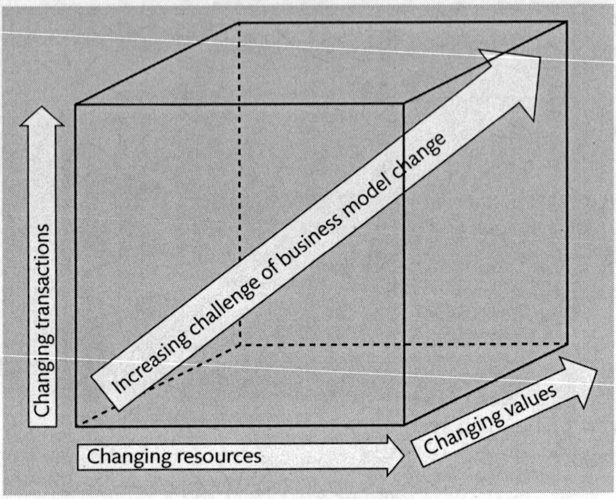

FIGURE 4.4 Difficulty of more complex business model change

that successfully implementing business model change required focusing the organisation on key capabilities, without losing sight of the larger market context. This can be a significant challenge. Similarly, business model change does not appear to be a learned skill – it does not get easier with practice.

Organisations can test and implement multiple business models

At one time, practitioners and management scholars believed that a company could have only one business model at a time. This is an extremely simplistic view of business models. The reality is that firms are in constant states of change and adaptation. The most sophisticated entrepreneurs and managers use this fluid perspective to test and adjust business model elements and even entire business models in real time. Very young ventures, especially new mobile apps or platform-dependent ventures, often test out a variety of business models before attempting to scale operations.

A great example of that is Ocere Ltd. In 2012, Tom Parling was growing his search engine optimisation (SEO) business, Ocere, with a combination of hustle and long hours. Founded in 2009, it had grown into an exciting venture in a rapidly evolving space. Ocere leveraged Tom's thorough understanding of Google's search algorithms and web-crawling systems to help Ocere's clients get more visibility in Google search results. But it was also an increasingly competitive and risky space, controlled almost entirely by Google's ability to adjust its search algorithms. By 2013, Tom could see that the company was too dependent on one-off projects and at risk of becoming irrelevant as the SEO industry consolidated. He began testing a number of other services related to internet searching and digital marketing. Each was, in effect, a business model experiment, conducted in real time with real resources, to explore the needs of real business customers in the confusing world of online marketing and sales. In less than a year, Ocere had found high-margin, high-customer-retention niche opportunities to provide product-specific leads to small services businesses around the UK. The company continues to grow one experiment at a time.

New business models are impossible to predict in advance

In hindsight, business model innovation may appear obvious. Consider the fall and rise of the music single. If we look back far enough, the majority of music sales were singles on 45rpm vinyl. The development of the 33rpm LP (long-playing record) started the 30-year dominance of album-based sales (vinyl LPs, cassette tapes, compact discs). With the advent of the internet, the cost of distributing digital content effectively dropped to zero. Suddenly it made sense again to sell music one song at a time. Today downloads of singles once again dominate the music industry, as shown in Figure 4.5. The biggest beneficiary of this innovation is neither musician nor music publisher. It is Apple, the company that launched iTunes®, the first online music distribution system linked to

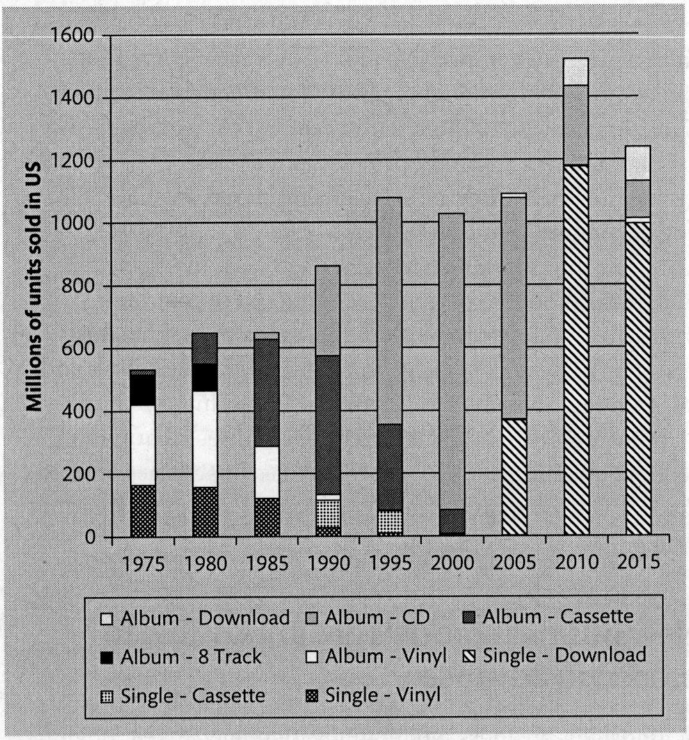

FIGURE 4.5 Music sales by type over time

Source: RIAA data and Minnesota Public Radio analysis, http://blog.thecurrentorg/2014/02/40-years-of-album-sales-data-in-one-handy-chart/

the major music publishing houses. Any of the major record labels could have done this, but they lacked the technical capabilities and the vision for how customers would access and use music in the digital economy.

RECAP

Congratulations on finishing Part 1 of the book! You know more about business models than the vast majority of managers and entrepreneurs. You understand the potential and the limitation of business model analysis. Here are the key ideas covered in Part 1:

- A business model is a way to explain how an organisation creates and captures value.
- A business model is a system that links organisational resources and activities.
- No one fully understands why some business models succeed and others fail.
- Creating a great business model is not easy.
- Innovative business models require going beyond traditional assumptions, obtaining data from customers and finding ways for the business model elements to work together.
- Innovative business models are high risk and high reward.
- Business models change, but changing business models requires insight, data and testing.
- Organisations can explore and test business models but, ultimately, business models have to be implemented in the real world.

You are now ready to start building business models from the ground up!

Part 2

Business model elements – the RTVN framework

In this section, we identify the three sides of business models and learn how they fit together. It helps to imagine a business model as a triangular pyramid that can be viewed from three different perspectives: resources, transactions and values. Combined, they form the core framework for business models. This approach can be used for any organisation, regardless of stage, size or type. Of course, the pyramid has a hidden side facing the ground. That hidden side is the business model narrative, the foundation of a business model's purpose and guide for evaluating inevitable trade-offs.

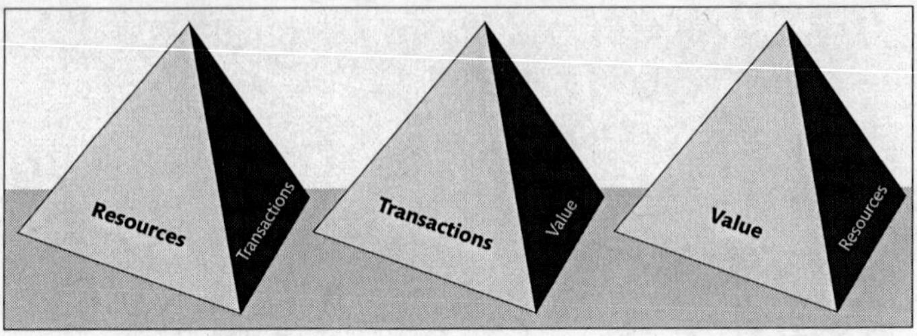

Three perspectives of a business model

Business models are *coherent* when the narrative links resources, transactions and values. Understanding coherence leads to business model maps and canvases. Once we have the design tools, the elements will also provide the framework for business model change and innovation.

5 Making resources work for your business

'The same products, services or technologies can fail or succeed depending on the business model you choose. Exploring the possibilities is critical to finding a successful business model. Settling on first ideas risks the possibility of missing potential that can only be discovered by prototyping and testing different alternatives.'

Alexander Osterwalder

Although business model analysis can begin anywhere, most managers and entrepreneurs start with resources. The resource structure is the most easily identified and concrete piece of the business model (Figure 5.1). Professional managers are used to thinking about resources as part of operational and strategic planning. The other perspectives are always there, but it is useful to analyse them one at a time.

Resources are all the 'things' that organisations use to create value. A 'resource-based view' of an organisation is a powerful perspective for understanding how and why some companies are strong competitors. The resources of the organisation are, in effect, the raw materials of a business model.

As you begin to explore, design, build and adapt business models, one of your own key resources will be a business model team. These could be colleagues, friends, advisors or other trusted experts. Your business model team helps you stay on track and develop creative ideas for your business model. Yes, there is a time investment to put the team together. But a team can build and assess business models much faster than one individual. In addition, a diverse team is much more likely to generate new and innovative business models than a solo entrepreneur or manager.

Business model resources

Business model resources types include assets, knowledge and capabilities. These types can also be characterised as tangible and intangible. Table 5.1 categorises organisational resources, including examples.

There are three steps to understand and assess the resource structure of a business model. First, the available and necessary resources must be inventoried, with careful attention to resource types. Second, resources must be assessed for creating business model value. Finally, we must consider whether the business model will effectively leverage and extend those resources.

Some guidelines help with resource structure analysis. First, not all resources are created equal. Even if we could put a

TABLE 5.1 Resource categorisation

Type	Tangible	Intangible
Assets	Equipment	Relationship with supplier
Knowledge	Steps and requirements for manufacturing process; intellectual property	Experientially based information
Capability	Consistently high manufacturing throughput	Consistently high manufacturing quality

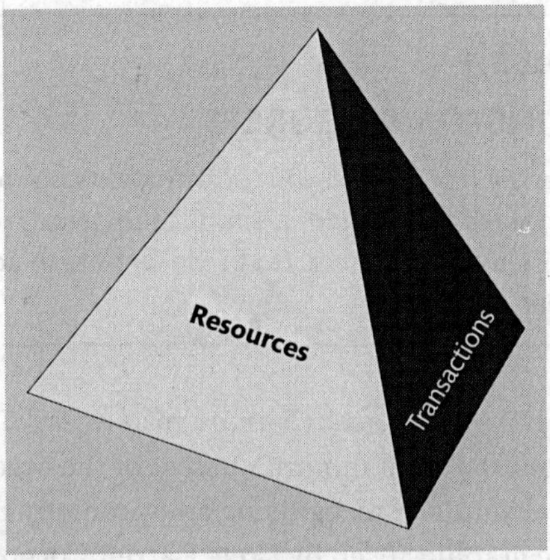

FIGURE 5.1 The resource perspective

clear value metric on every resource, it would not guarantee that comparisons are consistent and appropriate. Some resources, such as specialised capabilities or knowledge, take time to develop. Similarly, intangible resources may not be transferable.

Second, it is essential to assess the resource structure and how it interacts with the transaction and value structures. A common mistake in business model analysis is to focus on the specific value of one or two key resources.

Finally, it is a good idea to return to the resource structure after thinking about the transaction and value structures of the business model. Because most analyses start with resources, it is very common to miss key resources or resource interactions. For example, many business model analyses underestimate the importance of key customer or channel relationships. These are usually, and correctly, considered in the analysis of the transaction structure. At the same time, those relationships are also organisational resources. They may represent months, years or decades of effort. In many cases, the other resources of an organisation may have little or no value isolated from those relationships.

Worksheet 5.1

IDENTIFYING KEY RESOURCES

What are the key resources in your organisation's business model? Worksheet 5.1 provides a template to quickly identify and categorise those resources. Go to the website to access the worksheet.

A key question is: 'What about *human* resources?' Clearly, people are often the most important asset of the organisation. An excellent example of recognising and promoting this can be seen on the graphics used by Crete Carrier Corporation, a truck transport company based in Omaha, Nebraska. The company used the trucks themselves to identify that the driver was a critical organisational resource with an arrow pointing towards the cab and the statement: 'Our most valuable resource since 1937'. You can see examples of this on the website.

The importance of a single person may be especially critical at an early stage venture. For simplicity, however, it is often more effective to focus on the key knowledge or capabilities those individuals bring to the organisation. The knowledge and capabilities of that unique person usually can be identified and categorised into the resource grid. This is very important for business model analysis because (unfortunately) businesses cannot always rely on a unique individual to be available indefinitely. In addition, analysing the underlying information and capabilities that make someone indispensable may also help clarify how that person's time should be utilised in the business model.

Sometimes, the key resources seem obvious. Consider the case of Cellular Logistics, Inc. As a physiology PhD student at University of Wisconsin-Madison, Eric Schmuck developed a biological material that helps heal cardiac tissue. He formed a start-up company, Cellular Logistics Inc., in 2016 to commercialise that technology. By default, Eric is the most critical human resource at the venture – he knows the material better than anyone in the world. How does he fit into the Cellular Logistics business model? First, we need to understand that the patented material is technically the property of the university's technology transfer office. Eric's real value to the venture is the knowledge and capability associated with producing, testing and using the material. In addition, Eric is still learning about business management and technology venturing. He will significantly benefit from expert guidance and management mentoring to commercialise this complex innovation.

Do you have SHaRP resources?

Not every organisational resource is critical to a great business model. After all, many resources are common across organisations: paper, computers, internet access, writing skills, accounting, and so on. In other words, most resources are *necessary* but not *sufficient*. How can we tell? Based in part on research by management scholars, such as Berger Wernerfelt, Jay Barney, Richard Rumelt, Edith Penrose and others, we can identify the resource characteristics that make a difference.

Resources that build great business models are SHaRP: *Specialised, Hard to copy, Rare and Precious.*

Figure 5.2 shows how these combine in the resource perspective.

It is important to understand that there are gradations in these criteria, depending on the nature of the organisation. For example, in a high-growth technology company, the rarity and specialisation of the resources will need to be

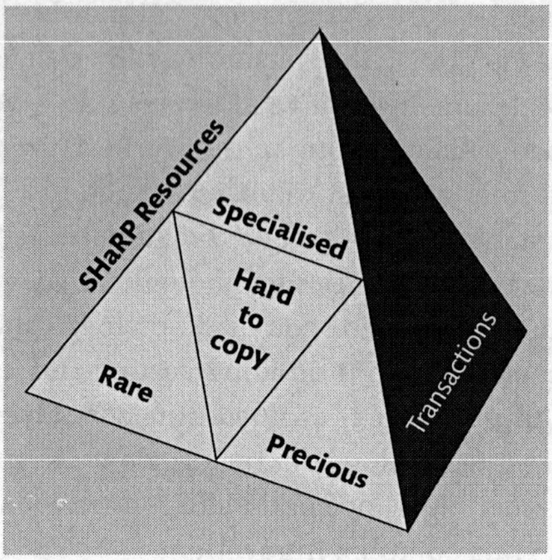

FIGURE 5.2 SHaRP resources for great business models

significant; a small, local retail shop will not require the same degree of uniqueness to be viable.

Specialised. Some organisational resources are common across business models. It is common sense that every organisation needs to be able to communicate, manage activities, track results and reward employees. The resources used to accomplish these universal objectives are generally common: paper, computers, human resource policies, and so on.

Some resources are very specialised. Patents and trade secrets are the classic examples. But sometimes resources are specialised because they are used in unique ways. Design and software engineering skills can be found at thousands of technology companies around the world. At Apple, those skills were trained up and deployed in a way to generate uniquely popular products that changed how people actually *used* technology products. For example, since around 2004, Apple's iPod® product line has captured roughly 75 per cent of the world's MP3 player market. Some of that success derived from protecting proprietary designs, but it was the original combination of design, software and understanding of music use that drove success. Keep in mind that the iPod® was neither the first MP3 player nor the least expensive option.

A great example of a specialised capability can be seen in the story of Adam Sutcliffe. His unique combination of human-centred design and insight into the challenge of hand sanitisation in clinical settings led to his innovation, the Orbel®. Sutcliffe used this sophisticated skill to develop a hand-sanitising system that relies on the human instinct to wipe hands on one's clothing. The Orbel™ is attached to clothing precisely where the hand rests, so that the wiping reflex results in sanitising the hands rather than transferring more germs onto them. You can read more about Sutcliffe and Orbel in the Human Design and Orbel Health Excursion at the book website.

Hard to copy. Some resources are difficult to copy or imitate. Trade secrets, such as the Coca-Cola® formula, generate a long-term resource value that is difficult to imitate. In most cases, however, resources that are difficult to copy stem from advantages in time or experience. Such resources traditionally may still be found in unique manufacturing configurations or processes. But they can also be observed in highly skilled labour capacities, organisational cultures and relationship management.

Rare. Some resources are simply rare. There is an inherent value in scarcity, but in a business model, resource rarity can refer to assets, unusual knowledge and unique abilities. A hospital might invest in a sophisticated imaging device, such as an magnetic resonance imaging (MRI) scanner. If no other hospitals or clinics in the area have a comparable device, that rare resource can be a valuable component of the hospital's operations. Of course, there need to be trained technicians to run the scanner and physicians to interpret the results. Rare resources are often most valuable in combination with other specialised (and sometimes rare) resources.

Many start-up technology companies rely on the scientific or engineering expertise of the key inventor. This is the case with Cellular Logistics. The technology innovator, Dr Eric Schmuck, is one of the only people in the world with the required knowledge and expertise on the culturing and manufacturing process for the company's proprietary biomaterial.

Rarity can also be relative. In the case of the hospital with the MRI scanner, rarity derives from local, not global, scarcity. There are other MRI scanners in the world; patients could receive MRI services by travelling far enough away. In addition, the hospital may have no control over the acquisition of MRI technology by other facilities. The same might be true for Cellular Logistics. The underlying cell culturing and manufacturing skills are not unique. Other people could be trained with the material. For Cellular Logistics, the *processes* are rare only because no one else has tried them. To maintain the rarity of the resource, Dr Schmuck will need to continue his own learning and skill building or *shift* his resource effort to other processes or capabilities that remain scarce.

You do not need to find specialised start-ups to see the power of rare and tacit capabilities. Incredible human skills are deployed regularly at many big, familiar companies. In the automotive industry, Toyota and Lexus have led the world in total quality management (TQM) and Six Sigma quality systems. Whilst TQM often emphasises automation and manufacturing design, there is still a role for sophisticated human senses. At the Lexus manufacturing plant that opened in 2015 in Kentucky, workers were trained to search for defects using their fingers. This is an example of a capability that crosses into the 'intangible' category. It can be trained by example and experience, but not learned from a manual or other traditional quality training tools. Workers learn by shadowing experts, combining objective information with subjective sense.

Precious. Some resources are simply more valuable than others. If you run a commission-based travel shop, some of the physical assets of the facility will support sales. Photos and souvenirs from exotic locations, models of cruise ships and testimonials from happy customers all lend legitimacy to the business. Computers and a fast internet connection are probably even more important, as customers will want to see current pricing, stateroom options and real-time information about weather and flights. In the end, however, the most precious skill may well be the selling capability of the salesperson who talks with the potential customer. How knowledgeable is that salesperson? Can she keep the customer engaged whilst looking up prices and options? Can she convince the customer to consider add-ons or upgrades? Does the customer feel excited or worried after making a down payment? The 'product' may include various arrangements for food, accommodations and transportation, but the most valuable salespeople are selling an experience, even before the holiday begins. The bottom line is that valuable resources are the foundation of viable products and services.

'You cannot business-model your way out of a shitty product.'

Tim O'Neill

Worksheet 5.2

HOW SHaRP ARE YOUR BUSINESS MODEL RESOURCES?

Go to the website and access Worksheet 5.2. What are the two or three key resources that drive the success of your business model? Use the SHaRP framework to assess those key resources. If your business is relatively small and/or simple, your resources only need to be SHaRP enough for local competition. But if you have significant growth aspirations, or your organisation will compete in a complex and changing environment, then you will want your resources to be as SHaRP as possible!

Relatively few resources will meet all the SHaRP characteristics. The more SHaRP characteristics, the more valuable the resource. Remember that resources are evaluated specifically for the organisation. To a soda can company, aluminium is just a commodity source material. To an aerospace company, specialised grades of aluminium might be the difference between an aircraft that flies and one that does not. Table 5.2 shows variants of one resource (information technology) to show how related resources may provide different value within a specific business model.

Let us look at Graze, which operates the largest US and UK direct mail snack food business, by sending customers a 'discovery box' to introduce them to wholesome snacks that are hand-picked and customised. You could also look at Hello Fresh, an international meal delivery service with a presence in several Western European and North American countries, as well as Australia. Both these companies are disrupting traditional grocery chain businesses, as well as shaping customer behaviour. On the face of it, the business model appears rather simple – you promote customised food, acquire customers through social media and marketing,

TABLE 5.2 SHaRP resources at a speciality clothing retail store

	Specialised	Hard to copy	Rare	Precious
Bar code scanner				
Buyer who knows fashion	X	X	X	X
Social media marketer	X			X
High end clothing brands		X		X
Book of repeat customers				X
Great location			X	X

and deliver customised products. Aha! But, dig a level deeper and you will start looking at the resources needed to make this model viable – where several others have failed with an online, subscription-based model. You need to be vertically integrated with the capacity to source, make and sell products directly to the end consumer, bypassing food retailers and controlling pricing. Then, you need to be great at handling operational complexity with bespoke food processing, packaging and fulfilment that needs to be designed, engineered and built for purpose. Finally, you need a deep learning artificial intelligence platform that connects, customises and adapts products to customer preferences in near real-time. These are SHaRP resources, which ensure you remain in business!

Leveraging and building resources in business models

Great business models do not just *use* resources. That would be like a football team that hires players for one match, assigns them randomly to positions and then releases them when the final whistle blows.

Great sports teams acquire and develop talent, leverage the specific skills and capabilities of those players to win games and learn from experience to further develop the talent base and team capability. Winning business models work the same way. The same model that leverages and exploits key resources should also build and develop those resources to make the business model more effective over time.

Some business models look good because a SHaRP resource can be exploited quickly. Quick kills can generate revenue and profit but are rarely sustainable. Creating a sustainable business model hinges on whether resources can be renewed and developed.

There are three key questions to ask about leveraging and building your business model resource structure. Keep in mind that it is much better to be honest and objective about the status of your business model resources. Your goal is to improve the overall business model, not pretend everything is just fine. Also, you may find that these questions can be answered more clearly when you have completed the business model analysis, including the transactive, value and narrative coherence parts of your business model.

- **Question 1: Does the business model tend to deplete or enhance your organisation's resources and capabilities?** Some business models naturally deplete the organisation's underlying resource base. Most manufacturing, inventory-based and service business models have a natural tendency to use up extant resources. Manufacturing equipment ultimately runs down, requiring repair or replacement. Manufacturing employees reach a maximum efficiency and eventually retire or otherwise leave the business. Service organisations rely on employees who often become dissatisfied with performing the same processes all the time. And, we are all familiar with the ongoing challenge of technology obsolescence.

  A few types of organisations see resource structure increase without *direct* significant effort. For example, high-quality wine may become more valuable with age. Of course, that presumes extensive work prior to storage. But we can at least imagine a business that buys high-quality wines simply for the purpose of storing them and selling them for a higher price in the future. Can you think of any business models that automatically increase the resource value of the human resources?

  Most organisations must expend effort to continually rejuvenate and build the resource structure. They invest in training, recruiting, maintenance and physical asset management.

The value of building and leveraging physical assets can be seen in successful organisations in any industry, no matter how specialised. You may not be familiar with Magic: The Gathering, a fantasy-based strategy card game, but there are roughly 20 million active players in the world. New cards are developed and distributed exclusively by Wizards of the Coast, now owned by Hasbro. There is a healthy secondary market for used cards, especially the rarer cards that are no longer produced or allowed in sanctioned tournaments. The most valuable cards regularly sell for more than US$10,000. There are now tens of thousands of unique cards. Knowing which cards are valuable, and assessing card quality, has become a rare capability, especially as the number of extant cards increases every year. Dan Bock (full disclosure: Dan is the author's brother) is the founder and manager of PowerNine Games, which deals exclusively in the secondary market for Magic cards. The company's eBay site has more than 25,000 auctions running. Dan has been asked by eBay and other resellers to use his unique and rare knowledge of MTG cards to identify fake cards. Over time, Dan has built an international reputation for his knowledge of Magic cards and expertise in their value. The business model of PowerNine starts with buying large collections of cards, often tens of thousands at a time. PowerNine disaggregates the collections and resells the cards on eBay. This ongoing process continuously enhances the capabilities of the company, ensuring that Dan and his team remain some of the most knowledgeable people in the world in this highly specialised area.

Question 2: Does the business model increase or decrease the value of your organisational partnerships and their resources?

A common flawed business model is a system that creates value by appropriating it from business partners and collaborators.

During the dot-com boom, hundreds of ventures were started that attempted to use the internet to connect suppliers and customers directly, circumventing existing distribution systems. This type of process is called 'disintermediation'. The key underlying assumptions were that (1) the extant distribution systems were inefficient, (2) the information necessary to facilitate purchasing decisions could be collected and disseminated effectively and (3) an independent third party was best positioned to create the necessary infrastructure and collect the rewards from a more efficient process.

FoodUSA.com (see Chapter 1) was an example of failed disintermediation. It extracted value from the food brokers whilst simultaneously threatening to impact the large food production companies. In theory, FoodUSA.com might have increased value for the participants in the industry. For example, the system might have enabled more effective pricing of processed meats, allowing producers to charge higher prices for higher-quality product. This could have been a case of increasing the size of the pie, which tends to benefit all participants. Instead, like most cases of disintermediation, the process threatened to move profits from the most powerful players to the least powerful. It is very rare for this type of disintermediation to succeed.

Question 3: What activities outside your business model build your resource structure?

Very often, the resource structure of the organisation can benefit from activities that seem otherwise unrelated to how the organisation creates value. These can, however, be tricky. The organisation may only see returns to such activities in the long run. Returns may only be accessible through the actions of other organisations or via processes outside the organisation's control.

An unusual example of this can be seen with Confederate Motorcycles. Confederate hand manufactures super high-end motorcycles in New Orleans. These are not bespoke; the company designs a cycle and then hand manufactures a limited run (usually fewer than 100) of the design. Customers pay anywhere from £50,000–£100,000 for a Confederate motorcycle, depending on design and run.

Confederate's target customers are ultra-wealthy collectors. Many store them indoors and treat them like museum pieces. Some ride them, but they certainly do not *race* them. Yet, every year, Confederate takes a motorcycle out to the salt flats in Utah and attempts to set a land speed record for their engine class. Why?

Going to the Utah salt flats builds the company's resource structure by developing internal capabilities related to design and production. But it also builds the company's intangible resources by simultaneously romanticising and concretising the vision that attracts ultra-wealthy customers in the first place. Learn more about Confederate Motorcycles in the Confederate Motorcycles and the Bonneville Salt Flats Excursion on the website.

Video resource

Confederate Motorcycles is a specialised manufacturer of small-batch, high-performance motorcycles. Watch these videos about the company and its founder, Matt Chambers. What business model elements, especially resources, are being referenced? Try to imagine rebuilding your organisation with some of the mindset and philosophy that drives Matt Chambers and the people at Confederate.

What can you take away from the Confederate Motorcycle story? Successful business models can be unusual and unexpected. Try to keep an open mind as you create and change business models. The most brilliant business models may require a completely different perspective than you have ever previously considered.

RECAP

- Most business model analysis starts with the resource perspective.
- Resources that comprise viable business models are SHaRP: *specialised*, *hard* to copy, *rare* and *precious*.
- Great business models develop and leverage, rather than deplete organisational resources.

6 Transactions in a business model

'You know your business model is broken when you're suing your customers.'

Paul Graham, co-founder of Viaweb and YCombinator

Nowhere is business model confusion greater than in transactions.

Early academic research on business models focused on transactions. As we have already discussed, a purely transaction-based approach to business models is extremely powerful. For better or worse, however, it has been superseded by a more practice-oriented approach. You can explore this in depth at the book website in the Transaction-Based Business Models Excursion at the book website.

Transactions connect the resources

The second side of the business model pyramid is the transaction-based perspective. Transactions are the connectors that link, combine and exchange resources in the value creation process. Sometimes these transactions are obvious; sometimes they are quite subtle or even hidden.

The most well-known examples of business model innovation and business model disruption are based on significant changes in the transactive structure of a business model. eBay, Priceline, Google's Adsense revenue model, iTunes® and Alibaba.com are all examples of industry-disrupting business model innovations driven by novel approaches to transactions.

As shown in Figure 6.1, there are three types of transactions in any business model. Internal transactions take place entirely within the organisation. These link people, groups, systems or any combination of these entities within the firm. External transactions take place entirely outside the organisation, but are linked to or associated with the organisation's value creating processes. Boundary-spanning transactions may sound exotic, but they are, in fact, the most familiar transaction type. Boundary-spanning transactions link something inside the organisation with something outside the organisation. These transactions span (cross) the organisation's boundary with the external environment.

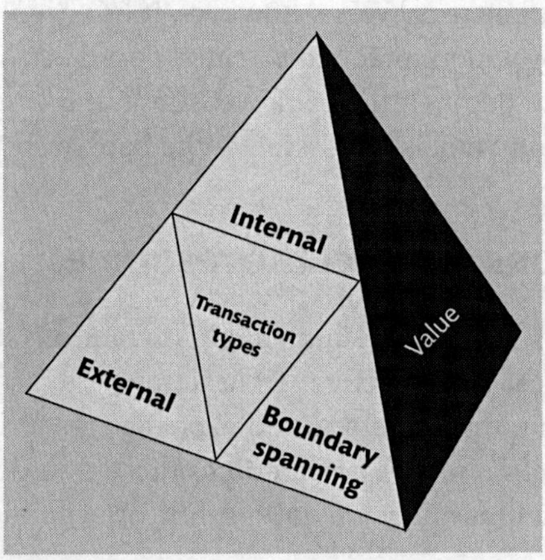

FIGURE 6.1 The transaction perspective of business models

Internal transactions

You may not have thought of it this way, but the majority of your organisation's transactions are internal. Managers often focus on transactions with external parties such as customers, partners, suppliers and even competitors. The reality is every organisational activity or process is a transaction – a connection or combination of internal resources. Internal transactions include hiring, manufacturing, meetings, and so on.

This perspective presents a challenge: which transactions are critical for business model analysis? Savvy managers focus attention on internal transactions that meet at least two of three criteria: necessary, highly specified and differentiating.

Necessary transactions seem straightforward. Surely, organisations only utilise internal transactions that are necessary?

Unnecessary internal transactions include wasted work as well as worthless activities. We hope the former are primarily cases of low employee engagement and poor human resource policies. The latter, however, often are directly tied to inefficient business models.

Worksheet 6.1

WASTED INTERNAL TRANSACTIONS AT YOUR ORGANISATION

Before reading further, go to the website and complete Worksheet 6.1 for your own organisation. What wasteful or low-value activities and transactions will you discover?

As organisations grow and change, once-important activities may become obsolete. Some organisational activities are generated as well-meaning but effectively unimportant busywork. In both cases, the output of the transaction tends to terminate with the specific people or groups involved.

Ask one question to identify and isolate internal transactions associated with inefficient business models: *Is the output of the transaction or activity utilised anywhere else in the organisation?* If the answer is 'no', then it is likely a wasted internal transaction.

We worked with a non-profit foundation that struggled with this problem. The volunteer trained on bookkeeping software left the foundation unexpectedly. One of the administrators began doing the bookkeeping in Excel because she didn't know how to use the bookkeeping software. Eventually, a new Treasurer transferred all the transactions into the accounting software. But the administrator continued to export data to Excel to generate periodic financial reports. Board members received, but did not use these reports because they were not in a standard form and did not always match the output from the bookkeeping software. In other words, the output of the internal transaction was a dead end.

Efficient and unique internal transactions help differentiate the organisation from competitors. At most organisations, there are a very small number of internal transactions that meet this requirement. Keep in mind that these are still *internal* transactions, so the differentiating effect must be obtained through other value creating activities. Does your organisation do anything internal so differently that it creates opportunities to be distinctive in the eyes of customers or partners?

A great example of leveraging internal transactions can be seen at PowerNine. Training employees is a key internal transaction: it exchanges the opportunity cost of time for skill development. At PowerNine, the leadership team train new employees to buy second-hand card collections differently from most other MTG card traders and sellers. Most of the small businesses in the industry have a 'buy list' of cards they will purchase for cash. This simplifies their transactions and keeps their per-transaction cost low. But PowerNine's founder, Dan Bock, realised that many card sellers wanted to offload entire collections in a single transaction. Everyone knows that most of the cards are *nearly* valueless, but a seller might have thousands of these nearly valueless cards, which may otherwise be simply thrown away.

So Dan trains employees to make an offer for *everything.* PowerNine does not miss out on card acquisition opportunities simply because a seller's most valuable card is not on the company's 'buy list'. This also ensures that nearly every seller at a given show or event talks to PowerNine during their selling process. This significantly increases the odds that the seller will talk to PowerNine again in the future. Dan knows that the most likely customer is someone who has been a customer in the past. The internal transaction of training employees differentiates PowerNine at the precise moment it matters the most, when a player wants to liquidate a collection.

The final characteristic is transaction specificity. Some internal transactions can be accomplished in multiple ways. In the case of the non-profit foundation, financial data could be generated from any number of bookkeeping systems and communicated to the board in numerous ways (e.g. electronic files, handouts, slides, verbal summaries). The entire bookkeeping process could be outsourced to an external service provider. In other words, the bookkeeping activities of the foundation are important, but not specific or differentiating to the foundation's business model.

Worksheet 6.2

IMPORTANT INTERNAL TRANSACTIONS

Worksheet 6.2 builds on the analysis from Worksheet 6.1. Identify 20 internal transactions and check them against the 'two of three' rule. How many of them should be addressed in your business model analysis? For most small- to medium-sized organisations, the odds are high that you will find you have narrowed your focus to fewer than 10 internal transactions. It is OK if you still have more than 10 (or, conversely, fewer than 5); take a moment to think about what this means for your business model. It might be that your organisation requires a more complex business model analysis, that your organisation has multiple business models or possibly that your organisation is undergoing business model change.

Boundary-spanning transactions

In business models, boundary-spanning transactions (BSTs) are where the action is. Boundary-spanning transactions connect the organisation to customers, partners, competitors and any other organisations or individuals outside the firm. A firm uses and leverages internal resources to *create* value; it develops and exploits BSTs to *capture* that value.

Basic BSTs include selling a product to a customer or buying materials from a supplier. To get to the heart of business models requires a much more sophisticated approach to boundary-spanning transactions.

If you are trying to assess, fix or innovate a business model and you do not know where to begin, start with the boundary-spanning transactions. The odds are good you will find the most salient issues, problems or opportunities here.

BSTs are most often associated with suppliers and customers. This is a remnant of value chain analysis that focuses on production inputs and outputs. Realistically, most firms have significantly more BSTs, though many of them are relatively undifferentiated.

This can be a critical challenge for many older and family firms. In a traditional framework, a small business had a close relationship with a bank. That relationship was often based on personal interaction with one specific banker. Such relationships represented an important BST for the firm, especially in situations where the firm needed quick access to capital.

Today, banking services are significantly more commoditised. Processes such as small business loans are generally subject to highly standardised review within financial institutions. In other words, for most small businesses, the financial BST has become a less critical component of the business model because the core services can be obtained from many financial institutions.

On the other hand, marketing, distribution and service channels have become significantly more important. The immediacy of communications, especially via online systems, has created opportunities and challenges for small businesses. Selling consumer products via large retailers (ASDA, Tesco, etc.) offers incredible economies of scale, but requires the firm to meet the operational and informational demands of the retailer. Distributing via online sites, such as Alibaba, Amazon or eBay, provides similar scale opportunities, but requires the firm to adapt to an information-rich and service-oriented interaction with customers. Similar effects can be seen in business-to-business supply chains, where communication and enterprise resource planning software provide deep and sophisticated connections between the firm and its various collaborators and partners. You can see more examples of BSTs in the BSTs in the IT Sector Excursion at the book website.

> **Worksheet 6.3**
> **BOUNDARY-SPANNING TRANSACTIONS**
>
> Go to the website and download Worksheet 6.3. You will identify the important BSTs for your business and draw how they are connected. The worksheet will help you explore the different individuals and organisations with which your firm transacts. These include customers, users, partners, suppliers, purchasers, experts, complementors and even competitors.

A powerful tool for better understanding transaction structure is a customer journey map. Exploring your customers' entire interaction with your organisation can be an eye-opening experience, leading to entirely new ways of thinking about your business model. The customer journey map can be used for almost any transaction, by changing your definition of the customer. After all, your organisation is the customer in your transactions with suppliers. If you have collaborative partnerships, then *both* entities are, technically, customers.

DBS Group in Singapore is an example of a traditional bank that transformed itself into the world's best digital bank by immersing itself in the fast-paced business culture in Asia. DBS re-envisioned itself as a 22,000-person start-up by specifically focusing on the customer journey. Every senior management team member had to participate in a customer journey to understand their experience, as well as finding ways to innovate the service so as to be engaged with the customer earlier and seamlessly before they purchase a service. For example, DBS launched the DBS Home Connect™ app. HomeConnect™ provides consumers with purchase histories of houses and other location-specific information, such as distance to transport and shopping facilities. The app embeds DBS into the customer journey well before a mortgage application decision. Similar shifts in the customer journeys for retail banking and wealth management meant that DBS was using fintech approaches to convert traditional, impersonal banking with the 'joy of banking'. By 2016, DBS started winning accolades as Asia's Best Bank and Aon Hewitt's Best Employer in Asia.

Video resource

You can see their CEO Piyush Gupta's views on banking industry transformation here.

External transactions

External transactions take place entirely outside of the organisation. These link people, groups and entities that are connected in various ways to your organisation. At the same time, they are sometimes so well-hidden or subtle that managers may be unaware of their role in a viable business model.

Consider this example. When you legally purchase a digital song or album, you make a payment to the distributor (e.g. Apple). If you listen to a song or album via a streaming service, you are indirectly paying the distributor (e.g. Spotify) either as a portion of your subscription fees or by listening to ads for free access. Companies like Apple and Spotify have broad licensing arrangements with the major music publishing companies (e.g. Sony and BMG) to share the revenue from these purchases. And the publishing companies have relationships with musicians and groups. Spotify's business model relies on those relationships, even though Spotify does not interact with most of the artists. From the artist's or publisher's perspective, your purchase is technically an external transaction because it happens outside their organisation and control.

What are the key external transactions for your organisation's business model? The odds are good that you could identify dozens of hundreds of transactions, especially if you traced each transaction to its full extent. Most, however, are not critical to the viability of your organisation.

For example, when we teach university courses, we rely on email to communicate with students. The number of transactions, people, systems and organisations associated with each email rapidly exceeds reasonable calculation. But these are neither specific to the business model of the university nor irreplaceable. You can find more examples of external transactions at the External Transactions Excursion on the book website.

Unfortunately, there is no simple, consistent way to identify the external transactions most important to your organisation. As you become more familiar with business model analysis, you may find this process becomes easier.

Worksheet 6.4

EXTERNAL TRANSACTIONS

Download Worksheet 6.4 from the website. It will give you useful guidance on trying to identify important external transactions.

Transactions frame value creation

Resources determine the value that your organisation *creates*; transactions frame the value that your organisation can *capture*. Capturing value is often much more difficult than creating it. Many entrepreneurs know exactly what they want to bring to market, whether it is a physical product or an intangible service. But just creating something with value does not mean that the organisation will actually capture it.

In fact, some entrepreneurs create value and allow that value to be captured by other individuals or organisations. Craigslist (USA) creates significant value through its online classifieds platform, but it captures that value only for very specific types of postings (e.g. apartments in San Francisco and New York). The value created by the platform is captured (or realised) by the users – people who post or reply to posts for other things in other locations. The same is mostly true for Gumtree, which was acquired by eBay in 2005.

Many start-ups, especially those with innovative technologies in traditional industries, struggle to capture the value they can create. In *Crossing the Chasm,* Geoffrey Moore describes the challenge of selling innovative products to the mainstream market. This is the case for most entrepreneurial firms, but innovative products in traditional industries are usually even more challenging. In traditional industries, markets are mature, and there may be few or no innovative or early adopter customers at all. Start-ups and young, unproven companies face a problem with transaction governance. The organisation has little or no legitimacy and the target customers incur a high cost in trust and compliance. If there is a problem with the product or service, the customer has little recourse because the start-up has limited options. Most startups do not have the resources to provide high levels of customer support. And, if the product or service fails, the customer is unlikely to recoup any losses.

Great examples of addressing these challenges can be seen in the parallel stories of Plumis (www.plumis.com) and Arctica. Plumis and Arctica were, effectively, sibling organisations. They were both formed through the Design London partnership between Imperial College London and the Royal College of Art. Both incorporated engineering and design research and were led by entrepreneurial students. And, most importantly, both were extremely innovative technologies entering very mature, traditional industries.

Plumis was commercialising a novel, mist-based fire suppression system. Arctica was commercialising a novel, low-power air-conditioning system. The fire safety and HVAC industries are heavily regulated and dominated by large, established companies. Both Plumis and Arctica created demonstration projects to highlight how their respective innovations addressed unmet customer needs. But neither was able to make progress on sales.

The Arctica team decided that market entry and growth would take too long; they negotiated an acquisition with a green-oriented engineering firm, Monodraught. This provided the founders with an opportunity to move on to other innovations and opportunities. The Plumis team decided to go it alone. They have successfully negotiated the various regulatory and industry hurdles to bring the Automist product to market. The value creation of the innovation is roughly the same, but it has taken five years to build the transaction system necessary to capture the value created for customers. There is no simple way to judge whether one choice was better than the other. Plumis and Arctica took different paths and have achieved different results.

Ultimately, transactions both drive and limit value creation. Keep in mind that value capture is more than revenue. Value may include information, positive emotions, brand identity, trust, etc. Is your organisation creating a lot of value but not capturing it? Then your boundary-spanning transactions are the right place to start. Who should benefit the most from the value your organisation creates? How does your organisation connect with those beneficiaries?

Designing transactions in business models

The transaction-based approach to business models is generally the least well understood. Yet the most well-known examples of business model innovation or business model disruption tend to be changes in transaction structure. Business model innovation can emerge from changing any of the business model components or a combination of components. But major disruptions usually reflect transactive changes. Apple won the MP3 download war by building relationships with the major music publishers and creating a legal distribution channel, not by generating its own new musical content or becoming a music publisher. Priceline did not build hotels; it offered a novel transactional model for hotel room bookings.

Evaluating transactions in business models is an important first step. But designing or redesigning transactions tends to be much more challenging. The good news is that, once you have been through the exercise, you are likely to feel more comfortable the next time around.

Unfortunately, there is no proven tool for redesigning business model transactions. The basic principles of various business design systems, like business process re-engineering, total quality management (Six Sigma), activity analysis and just-in-time systems can be helpful. At the same time, they tend to emphasise primarily internal processes with a focus on efficiency rather than innovation.

A brute-force approach is, for most organisations, also unlikely to be helpful. Endless lists of the firm's transactions probably will not generate clear and compelling insight into new or improved transaction systems.

Completing one or more of the canvas mapping activities (Chapters 9–12) may be sufficient for (re)designing your business model transaction structure. If, however, you discover that your canvases tend to be strong on resource and value innovation but rather mundane with regard to transactions, then some additional intervention is probably warranted. We recommend the following three-step process for tackling this important challenge.

Step 1: draw your transaction model

A good starting point is to simply draw out the key transactions in whatever type of diagram works for you. A flow chart, box and arrow diagram or a freeform sketch might do the trick. Start with your organisation at the centre and then draw out the key transactions that determine how value is captured. Some will be easy. Who pays you? Who do you pay? What other key partnerships drive your organisation's day-to-day activities? Where does key information about markets come from? When in doubt, write it down. You can always move it or cross it out later.

A mindmap might be a useful way to draw your transaction structure. There are many free online mindmapping tools. Googling 'online mind map' should generate numerous options, such as MindMup, MindMeister, and Coggle. We have encouraged students to use these with excellent results.

Step 2: identify pinch points

Now that you have a diagram (you did do a mindmap or schematic, right?), you need to think about the pinch points. Your goal is to figure out the three to five specific transactions that are limiting your business model in some way. You probably already have some suspicions – now is the time to document them as hypotheses or intuitions.

From there, you might try asking the following questions:

- Which transactions utilise the most organisational resources?
- Do any transactions have hidden governance policies or governance policies that are unclear or unspecified?
- Is there significant overlap across important transactions? Do some transactions only take place when other transactions have failed or are unintentionally neglected?
- Which transactions tend to require extensive monitoring and/or remediation?
- Are there transactions that could be eliminated without directly impacting value creation or value capture?

Step 3: explore different transactions

As noted previously, designing new transaction structure, content and governance is usually the most difficult element of business model (re)design. Do not be discouraged if you find this to be the case!

Sometimes, of course, transaction (re)design just leaps out at you. Sometimes, the process of careful drawing and unpacking leads logically to addressing certain transactions. If this happens, the needed modifications become obvious.

A good example of transaction re(design) can be seen in the satisfaction survey used by Hampton Inn and Suites. Hampton Inn and Suites is a subsidiary of the Hilton Hotels and Resorts Company. Based primarily in North America and Europe, the 2,000+ properties in the chain offer accommodation targeting business travellers and families. After staying at a Hampton Inn, customers are encouraged to take an online survey about their experience. One of the questions in the survey is, 'During your stay, were you aware of the Hampton Inn and Suites 100% satisfaction guarantee?' This is an effective mechanism to reveal transaction governance to customers in a positive way. It is possible that customers reporting problems might see this as either an opportunity to claim a refund or a reason to try a Hampton Inn hotel again. In either case, it provides a mechanism to remediate a poor customer experience. Satisfied customers likely perceive that they made a good choice.

Transaction (re)design

Sometimes, the three-step process for transaction design is not enough. It can be difficult to imagine changing specific transactions or the overall transaction process, especially when ingrained and familiar.

There are many high-level transaction (re)design approaches to change how you think about transactions at your organisation. Table 6.1 shows an even dozen.

TABLE 6.1 High-level transaction (re)design approaches

Disintermediate	Extend
Simplify	Virtualise
Combine	Unpack
Outsource	Eliminate
Expose	Hide
Update	Integrate

Specific details and guidance for these are provided at the BMB website in the Transaction (re)Design Excursion. Whether or not the three-step process gave you useful direction in transaction design, this list could help jumpstart your thinking about new approaches to the transactions in your business model. Each possibility represents a means to change the way you think about your organisation's transactions. This is a great opportunity to draw on the expertise and creativity of your business model team.

RECAP

- The transaction perspective to business models is both very powerful and somewhat challenging.
- The most exciting business model changes and innovations tend to involve novel transactional systems.
- Great business models address internal, external and boundary-spanning transactions.
- Designing transactions benefits from a map or drawing, identifying pinch points and exploring alternatives.

7 Designing business models for value

'Many startups . . . start focusing way too early on their business model, especially what their various sources of revenue will be, what their sales channels will be, and what their costs will be, and they leave the pesky matter of "the solution" – can they actually solve the target customer's problem by discovering a solution that is valuable, usable and feasible – as a . . . task for later.'

Marty Cagan, Silicon Valley Product Group

Corporate strategy is about value compared to competitors. Business models are about *absolute* value. A viable business model generates value, full stop.

When we talk about the value dimension of business models, we are discussing the deep mechanisms and systems that underlie the foundation of nearly all organisational activity. Organisations exist to accomplish goals that cannot be executed by individuals alone. We therefore need to consider the issue of business model *value* as an outcome of organisational *design*.

The role of design in great business models

The elements of an organisation are connected in a design. The prior chapters have been leading to this: the elements are the resources, the connectors are the transactions. The design of the organisation is the logic or system that yields valuable outcomes.

There are really two components of business model design. The first is the value dimension – how the business model creates and captures value. When resources and transactions are fit for need and well deployed, the design creates value. The second, which we will discuss in Chapter 8, is the business model narrative.

Why do we bother with this? Most entrepreneurs and managers do not actively or purposely *design* the business model for their organisation. They just put nose to grindstone and get to work!

Most business models do emerge by necessity without formal design planning. The general consensus amongst business model scholars and practitioners, however, is that purposeful design helps ensure the business model accomplishes what was intended. In other words, the *process* of designing the business model increases the likelihood that the organisation creates real value.

The design process provides insight into a variety of business model details that might otherwise be missed. Is there synergy or conflict amongst business model resources? Are the transactions organised to extract and exploit the most value from the resources?

'The process by which firms design the business model can, in and of itself, create enormous value.'

Professor Raphael Amit, Wharton School of Business

For a given set of resources and transactions, there may be one viable business model, or there could be dozens, hundreds or more. Change one element and the set of possible designs changes.

This is especially relevant in under-developed markets and industries. It was true for many types of information technology services in the late 1990s and early 2000s. It remains true in industries such as artificial intelligence and regenerative medicine. In such cases, optimal design cannot be *discovered* because, arguably, it does not yet exist. Instead, effective business model designs must be *created,* often with the help of intuition, and *tested,* using an experimental approach.

In business model design thinking, nothing is set in stone. If a specific business model element or transaction appears to be both a problem and yet essential, try eliminating it to explore alternative business model designs.

Recognising stakeholders

The first step in business model design is recognising stakeholders.

Stakeholders are individuals or organisations with a beneficial interest in the organisation's production activities. The most commonly referenced stakeholders are customers and investors, with employees often a distant third. The reality is there are almost always more stakeholders, as your transaction schema in Chapter 6 should have revealed. In addition, the order of importance of those stakeholders is not set in stone.

The global leader in email marketing delivery, Return Path, was founded on a reordering of stakeholder interest. Return Path explicitly identifies its employees as its primary stakeholders. As stated in their 'Who We Are' video: 'We put our customers second . . . because we put our employees first.' This was a core principle of the firm's business model from the moment it was founded. Founder and CEO Matt Blumberg stated, 'I would not run a business that I would not want to work at.' This total rearrangement of the stakeholder ordering has been a driving factor in nearly every aspect of the company's growth and success. Blumberg's blog describes and explores how this reordering has driven the culture of the business. Making that culture explicit reveals the other core values of the organisation.

Exploring stakeholders exposes important business model assumptions and expectations. You can read more about information and value design in the Information-Sharing and Value Design Excursion on the BMB website.

Let us consider how a business model can be altered radically based on stakeholder priorities. Professor Miron Livny is a globally recognised expert on distributed computing. In 1988, he developed a system for high-throughput computing on distributed resources. Now called HTCondor™, the system incorporates more than 450,000 hosts and more than 3,000 pools worldwide.

When Livny first launched Condor, he could have applied numerous value prioritisations. For example, he could have identified himself as the primary stakeholder and either used the software as a basis for consulting services or formed a start-up company to commercialise the system.

Instead, Livny saw the *world* as his stakeholder. In his mind, the world had growing needs for inexpensive processing power. To make this possible, he retained the software as an ongoing research project within the university, relying on open source architecture. His 'organisation' does not generate profits because financial returns are turned into scholarships and university research projects. The value capture process uses money as an *intermediate step,* rather than the final metric. You can read more about Livny and the Condor story in the Condor Excursion on the BMB website.

Worksheet 7.1

IDENTIFYING STAKEHOLDERS

Go to the website and download Worksheet 7.1. In this worksheet, you will identify key stakeholders and allocate value across them. This will help reveal your assumptions and expectations for your business model as it currently exists.

Intangible value

Intangible value creation and capture is often a key, unrecognised element of a successful business model. Intangible resources, capabilities and value are usually much more difficult for competitors to copy, acquire or expropriate.

Table 7.1 provides a simple typology of intangible resources and value based on the research of Fernandez, Montez and Vasquez. The typology has been adapted to emphasise the link between intangible resources and value capture.

One of the most high-impact business model design activities is identifying both tangible and intangible sources of value. The vast majority of businesses, small and large, incorporate intangible value into their business models. For example, many family businesses strive to create and maintain well-paying jobs for family members; some family businesses operate with this as the primary goal.

TABLE 7.1 Intangible resources and value

Resource unit	Category	Examples	Value creation	Value capture
Individual	Human capital	Generic knowledge Specific knowledge	Unique activities and processes	Service premiums, product premiums
Organisation	Organisational capital	Norms and rules Routines Culture Organisational memory	Efficient activities and processes	Low HR turnover, low operational costs
Organisation	Technological capital	Intellectual property Databases	Information advantages	Product premiums, customer lock-in
Organisation	Relational capital	Reputation Brand Loyalty Relationships	Low coordination costs	Long-term relationships

Worksheet 7.2

TYPES OF VALUE

Download Worksheet 7.2 from the book website. Carefully assess the various types of value that your organisation creates for all its shareholders. How many of those are tangible? How many are intangible? The worksheet might help you identify intangible values that you have not previously made explicit.

Creating and capturing value in business models

Ultimately, a business model works only if it creates and captures value. Value bound up in resources and transactions must be *realised* and *secured* for the organisation to benefit, survive and thrive. This is a very good time to step back, take a deep breath and try to think at a very high level about your organisation or venture. Think about the following questions:

- What value does the organisation create?
- How is that value captured?
- If the creation or capture are not what you intend, or could be improved, what would need to change?
- Is this a business model problem, or is it really an operational or implementation problem?

This is not to say that an organisation must create 100 per cent of all potential value or capture 100 per cent of all created value. In fact, many organisations purposely allow for inefficient value creation and/or capture. These apparent inefficiencies may reduce coordination costs or facilitate value capture by other entities, to the benefit of your organisation in the long run.

If you have been doing the various activities and worksheets in this book, you have probably already thought of numerous possible changes to your business models. This is the right time to consider whether any of those changes could improve value creation and capture. As we will discuss later in the book, the only way to be sure is to run experiments.

Designing for value

Raphael Amit is one of the top business model scholars in the world. He worked with IDEO, a world-renowned creative design company, to generate a business model design process. The business model design process developed by Amit and IDEO is shown in Figure 7.1.

All business model implementation should lead to the desired value creation and capture goals. If you cannot link the business model creation process to the value creation and capture you want, then there is a fundamental flaw in your business model.

Observation

Designing a business model for value begins with observation about value creation. What is the value being created currently? What value could be created? How is value being captured or appropriated?

One powerful tool for understanding how value is really created for customers is *empathic design*. Empathic design is about observing how people and organisations actually use your product or how they actually function *without* your

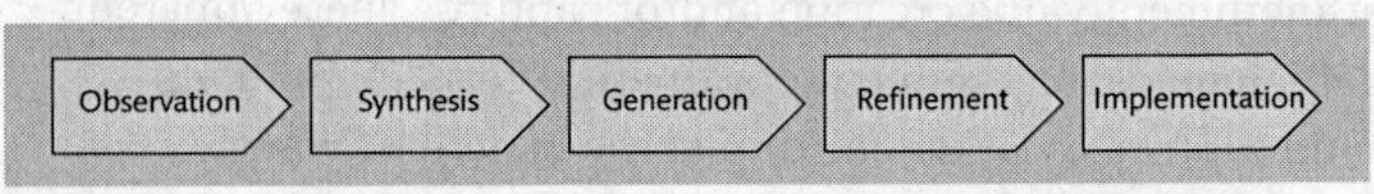

FIGURE 7.1 Amit and IDEO business model design process

product. Remember, just because your innovation is new, or even better than what is already out there, does not mean that customers will automatically buy it. There may be many reasons why customers will choose not to buy your product, even if it is better.

If your potential customers live without your product or service now, you need to understand how and why they live without it. Once you observe and understand how they live without it, you will be much closer to figuring out what you need to offer so they cannot live without it.

'For every hour you are spending on R&D activities, you should be spending one hour actually talking to your current or potential customers.'

Mark Daugherty, serial entrepreneur (personal interview, 2015)

Synthesis

Synthesising the observational data that you have gathered might be straightforward. In some cases, current customer behaviour fits reasonably well with your intended product offering and an obvious business model.

A good example of this is a small restaurant in Madison, Wisconsin (USA) called Short Stack Eatery. Co-founders Alex Lindenmeyer and Sinead McHugh observed the popularity of breakfast items at restaurants in the downtown Madison area. Madison's high density of university students and emerging café society create demand for non-traditional food options. Students and other downtown visitors often want breakfast food during non-breakfast hours. The solution: a restaurant, serving only breakfast foods, open for 88 consecutive hours, from 7 am on Thursdays to 11 pm on Sundays. Lindenmeyer and McHugh shifted the business model challenge from a food choice issue to a human resource challenge: staffing/managing 88 continuous hours of service.

In this case, the question and answer were straightforward, if a bit unusual. As the Short Stack Eatery website states: 'Why doesn't Madison have this? It was a simple question that we didn't have an answer for . . . Over the next three and a half years, we worked and reworked every detail: simple, fresh and local breakfast. All the damn time.'

Not every business model can be so simply designed for value based on customer and user observations. The innovation underlying Orbel Health combined direct observations of hand sanitation practices in hospitals and human behaviour-centric design. Sutcliffe then brought prototypes back to hospitals to see if and how nurses and doctors would actually use them. The nurses and doctors who tried the product liked it so much that they attempted to keep the prototypes! The synthesis of observation, prototyping and data collection showed that the need was real.

Generation

Generating possible business models is primarily a creative process. In some cases, it requires developing a very detailed and comprehensive map. In *Business Model Generation,* Alexander Osterwalder proposed the Business Model Canvas for this purpose. We will devote Chapter 11 to using the Business Model Canvas for growth-stage firms.

Many organisations, however, should use simpler tools and processes to generate business models, especially during the early stages of the design process. Chapters 9 and 10 provide simpler frameworks for pre-launch and start-up firms. Weill and Vitale's *Place to Space* also provides a great framework for generating business models, especially in information technology and online businesses.

If you are truly starting from scratch, a useful starting point is a simple list of business model types. There are a variety of such lists out there, but one of the more comprehensive versions was created by Accenture when business models were just entering the mainstream vocabulary. The broad types are grouped into categories: price, convenience, commodity-plus, experience, channel, intermediary, trust and innovation. Each category has multiple business model examples.

We do not believe that this typology includes every possible business model, nor do we think that all the business models described are necessarily unique. If you are just getting started with business models, the Accenture list can be a good starting point. It may help you identify possible models and eliminate unlikely models.

Some observations should be made about the typology and the critical business model dimensions.

First, the majority of business models in the Accenture report rely primarily on strength in the resource structure. That should not be a surprise – it is the most familiar structure and has been developed extensively within the field of corporate strategy. Second, as we already discussed, many disruptive business models that you might recognise from the internet revolution are transaction-dominant. Newer internet models, such as 'freemium' and even 'tip jar' models, could be considered intermediary or even trust models and still focus primarily on transactive structures.

Finally, value-driven business models are the most rare. Why? Because value in a business model is always a necessary factor for viability. The value creation mechanisms for most business models have been tried and tested. The determining factors for success in many newer business models rely on specialised resources or transaction efficiency. Only a few business models downplay resource and transaction differentiation and rely entirely on distinctive value structures. Our opinion is that Google is the best example of this; you can read more in the Excursion on Google at the BMB website.

Worksheet 7.3

THINKING ABOUT BUSINESS MODEL TYPES

Go to the website and download Worksheet 7.3. Unlike most of the other worksheets, this one is primarily a reference for you. It summarises the business model types and examples from the Accenture report and notes which business model dimension (resource, transaction, value) is most critical. Which model is most like the organisation you run or are planning to launch? Are there similar models on the sheet that might be better?

Refinement

At this stage of business plan creation, refinement is more about excluding alternatives and options than getting all the details right.

Start with the tentative identification of your intended business model. If you did not select one of the business models from Worksheet 7.3, either select one or create your own variant in a sentence or two.

You should now try to answer a short set of questions about that choice compared to similar options. The full set of detailed questions can be found on Worksheet 7.4.

Simple questions to refine your business model:

1. How do your *customers* describe the value they obtain from your organisation?
2. What assumptions about your value creation lock you into your current business model? Write down at least

three assumptions. How could you change or abandon some of those assumptions to create more value for your customers?

3 Think back to these last three chapters about resources, transactions and value. Go back to your SHaRP resources analysis, your transaction model drawing, and your list of tangible and intangible values. How do all these fit together?

> **Worksheet 7.4**
>
> **REFINING THE DRAFT BUSINESS MODEL**
>
> Download Worksheet 7.4 from the BMB website. Read and answer the detailed questions to refine your tentative business model. Remember that none of this is set in stone, so try to be as open-minded and creative as possible.

Implementation

The final step in designing a business model for value is, of course, implementing the design. Step-by-step instructions on implementing business model design is beyond the scope of this book for three reasons. First, every business model is implemented slightly differently. Second, business model design implementation also depends heavily on the stage of organisational development and how much business model change (rather than creation) is required. Finally, implementation is necessarily a fluid process, which should include a certain amount of experimentation and adaptation.

For the moment, keep the following touchpoints in mind about business model implementation:

- Clearly describing the business model elements will facilitate communicating it to organisational participants and change agents.

- Putting a (new) business model into place requires that the resource, transaction and value structures complement each other.
- Our research has shown that business model innovation and change is best led by a single person rather than by a committee or team.
- Implementing a (new) business model requires focusing on some areas of the organisation more than others; the implementation process will require delegating some functions to other trusted entities or partners.

The business model design process starts with observation and concludes with implementation. But this is only one step in the overall business model cycle. If you are launching a new venture or considering significant business model change, you will likely start this process more than once before settling on implementation. Business model design is rarely a linear process. Designing for business model value requires creativity and flexibility. Implementing for business model value requires adaptability to translate design into new activities within the organisation.

At this point, you have thought about SHaRP resources, drawn a map of your transactions and carefully considered value creation from multiple angles. You have also honed your general management skills associated with strategy, operations and supply chain management.

One of the reasons that business models are so compelling, however, is because truly brilliant business models go beyond operational activities and strategic management. In the next chapter, we will address the most challenging business model perspective: narrative.

RECAP

- Great business models address both tangible and intangible value.
- Value has to be created and captured.
- The value perspective shows how resources and transactions are connected in the design of the organisation.

8 Narratives and business model storytelling

'Completing a business model and identifying its critical parts is only that first step, the hard part is getting it off the "drafting board" and making it something tangible and potentially commercially viable for those around you to engage with.'

Paul Hobcraft

Business models are unique because they require a narrative. A great business model tells a coherent, convincing and executable *story.*

Entrepreneurs and managers embraced the business model because it appealed to their sense of intuition. A great business model can be quickly and clearly communicated to everyone, inside and outside the organisation. Viable business models have to make sense: to you, your organisation and your customers and users.

'The problem is that many times people suspend their common sense because they get drowned in business models and Harvard Business School teachings.'

Mo Ibrahim, founder of CelTel

In this chapter, we will explore the power and pitfalls of business model narratives. We will explore the specific challenges of aligning organisational elements and processes with a business model story.

Business model narratives connect the other elements

A narrative approach to business models is valuable for many reasons. First, business models are *meant* to be communicated. Business model narratives help ensure that organisational purpose is consistent and compatible with the other business model elements. Second, narrative is a critical tool for building organisational legitimacy. Finally, business model narrative can be used to change the organisation's environment.

You might be asking: 'Why doesn't business model analysis start with narrative? Why not build resources, transactions and value *around* the narrative?'

In fact, many entrepreneurs do start with the narrative. We are addressing it last for two reasons. First, we suspect many readers already run an organisation, so generating a new 'story' from scratch would be difficult or awkward. Second, good stories do not guarantee good business models. If you'd like to think further about this, please see the Starting with Narrative Excursion at the book website.

Here are some great examples of the narratives that led to interesting business models:

- 'Hand sanitisation is a critical problem in health care settings. What if I could use deeply ingrained human behaviour to drive, instead of inhibit, hand cleaning?' (Orbel)

- 'Data for predicting rail track failure needs to be updated regularly – as frequently as heavy freight trains use the track, if possible.' (MRail)
- 'Email spam hurts everyone – users and legitimate senders of email marketing messages. It costs almost nothing for spammers to update and send spam email. Instead of trying to blacklist an ever-changing set of email words and malicious senders, let's create a whitelist of verified legitimate senders.' (Return Path)

A narrative has a plot

Business models are meant to be communicated. The most effective form of human communication is a story. Think about the last few conversations you had with your colleagues, friends and family. How many of those involved storytelling?

Stories are effective communication tools because they rely on a set of universal components and structures. We will not dive into the depths of literary criticism or cultural anthropology here, but we will reference some key elements of the narrative paradigm.

One component of the narrative paradigm is the idea that all stories can be grouped into a limited number of plots. One useful, if controversial, typology of plots was proposed by Christopher Booker. These include 'Rags to Riches', 'Voyage and Return', 'The Quest', and so on. Take a look at the Booker's Narratives Excursion at the book website to see the full list.

A corporate strategy is also a story, but it is fundamentally a story of struggle – how the firm will compete against rivals. In other words, a strategy story is about defeating competitors. As Booker might say, it is an 'overcoming the monster' story.

By contrast, a business model tells a story in which a problem is solved (value creation) through interactions with various other entities (transactions) via the judicious use of assets and capabilities (resources). A business model can fit any one of the basic narratives.

What is your organisation's basic business model plot? Why does the organisation exist in the first place? How has it grown over time? What do you hope it will accomplish in the next two to three years?

> **Worksheet 8.1**
>
> **YOUR ORGANISATION'S STORY**
>
> Download this worksheet from the website and explore your organisation's story. Would your employees recognise that story?

Narratives create legitimacy

A business model narrative does more than just connect the other business model elements. It provides a compelling story that legitimises the firm's activities and goals to external stakeholders such as customers, competitors and partners. Organisational legitimacy means that internal and external stakeholders share a consensus that the organisation's intents and goals match its behaviours. In effect, the organisation needs to 'walk the walk'.

Legitimacy validates a shared culture, a framework for understanding and evaluating what actually happens at the organisation. A business model narrative is one of the most powerful mechanisms to generate legitimacy. It establishes a shared story that is easily communicated and understood by employees and managers and, ultimately, external stakeholders as well.

Business model narratives drive internal organisational alignment. An effective business model narrative should make sense to internal stakeholders. Share your narrative with a few key employees. They should respond to the narrative by saying something like: 'Yes, that is the story of the organisation.' If not, you have a problem already.

Return Path is a great example where internal narrative was critical. Return Path is the world's leading email marketing tools and whitelisting company. Return Path built a business model narrative about being 'the good guy' in the email marketing space. Email marketing is a legitimate service that is badly abused. Consumers and companies suffer because the majority of email is spam.

Return Path founders and executives had spent years developing this narrative. Employees had bought into it. But one aspect of the company's email marketing system unintentionally allowed certain types of spam emails to be identified as 'safe'. Technically, Return Path was simply implementing the 'fine print' rules for email marketing that most consumers do not read. In fact, Return Path was generating revenue from some of its customers because of this policy.

The executive team chose to make the situation transparent to the employees. Should Return Path continue to implement the rules that everyone had agreed to, even though it resulted in spam emails getting to end users? Or should it close the loophole and risk giving up revenue? What would you do?

The response from employees was clear and compelling. Return Path was a 'white hat'. The business model of the company had always been predicated on 'Doing the right thing'. Employees identified with the narrative of being 'email heroes'. They overwhelmingly wanted the company to close the loophole, even if it meant giving up revenue, even if it meant jeopardising the company's growth plan. Choosing to do the wrong thing was not part of Return Path's business model narrative. The narrative was consistent.

Return Path terminated that product.

Using narrative to change the environment

Business model narratives reach beyond the boundaries of the firm. Business model legitimisation can change or even create entire industries. The stories told by entrepreneurs during industry upheaval generate entirely new practices. Entrepreneurs who legitimise those practices in the broader environment acquire the resources they need, such as venture capital.

Craigslist and Google are two of the most compelling examples. Craigslist demonstrated that multi-sided markets could be inexpensively bridged with online platforms. In other words, people could trade goods and services directly with only passive support. Google demonstrated that the cost of many online services could be sustained by advertising rather than subscriptions, enabling vast data collection processes via user activity. The legitimisation of these and other experiments resulted in the explosion of online ventures and systems that drive nearly all internet-based commerce and communication.

Craigslist provides one of the most fascinating examples of a narrative that works from some audiences but not others. It has revolutionised the classified advertising market. The site is one of the top 20 in the US and top 100 in the world for total traffic. But it monetises only a fraction of that traffic, prompting some industry observers to describe its business model as 'insane'. But the narrative of Craigslist was never about profit maximisation, as noted by the company's CEO, Jim Buckmaster. There was always an intent to create value for the everyday users of the site. In this narrative, the value lost by newspapers has been dwarfed by the volume of low-cost transactions that benefit private parties and would not have happened otherwise.

Most organisations do not create a business model narrative

Generating compelling business model narratives should be straightforward. Yet, most organisations simply do not bother. Instead, many write mission, vision or value statements. These are, generally speaking, also useful. But mission and vision statements primarily emphasise the aspirations of the organisation. And value statements (should) emphasise the core beliefs of the key founders or owners. None of these addresses the business model: how the firm is designed to generate value.

Many start-ups (and other firms) generate elevator pitches. The 10-, 30- or 60-second elevator pitch is somewhat closer to the business model narrative. An elevator pitch usually includes a summary of the organisation's value proposition. The purpose of the elevator pitch, however, is to excite someone who previously has never heard of the organisation. It is a *pitch* that sells the possibility of the idea or venture. A good business model narrative can be the basis of an effective elevator pitch. If the business model is attractive and convincing, other people, including investors, would want to hear more.

'[Business models] are, at heart, stories – stories that explain how enterprises work. A good business model answers Peter

Drucker's age-old questions: Who is the customer? And what does the customer value? It also answers the fundamental questions every manager must ask: How do we make money in this business? What is the underlying economic logic that explains how we can deliver value to customers at an appropriate cost?'

Harvard Business School Associate Joan Magretta

Crafting a business model narrative

The three elements of a business model are straightforward: resources, transactions and value. The narrative ties them all together. A business model narrative should explain, clearly and concisely, how an organisation conducts transactions to generate value from its key resources.

Try and generate one for your organisation or venture, making sure that you build in all of the necessary components. Note that this may not be as easy as it sounds. As with most aspects of business model analysis, practice will help.

Worksheet 8.2

CRAFT A BUSINESS MODEL NARRATIVE

Download this worksheet from the BMB website. Use what you learned from Worksheet 8.1 to craft a business model narrative.

Let us take a more careful look at MRail so we can see how a business model narrative is formed and changed.

MRail's vertical track deflection measurement system sounds very complicated. In reality, it is both simple and incredibly clever. Shane Farritor, Professor of Mechanical Engineering at the University of Nebraska, recognised that railroad track does not generally fail whilst unused. Instead, it fails when heavy freight trains pass over it. A loaded coal hopper weighs approximately 120,000 kg (263,000 pounds). As you might guess, the strain on the rail and the ground below is enormous, especially when hundreds of cars pass over the track segment at 100 km/h. If the ground or the rail is weak, the steel rail will deflect downwards as the wheels pass over. Too much deflection and the rail will deform or break. If the track fails, the result will be an incredibly costly train accident.

Farritor realised that the trick would be to measure the deflection constantly, rather than at static track locations. In other words: mount the measurement system on the train so it measures track deflection continuously. He acquired an old rail car, built the laser measurement system on it, and convinced rail operators to attach the car to the end of freight trains like an extra caboose. As the trains hauled the modified car around, Farritor recorded track deflection data for thousands of miles of track. In the succeeding years, he demonstrated that derailments were happening precisely at the locations where his system identified more significant track deflection.

Here is one possible narrative for the business model MRail first considered. The specific elements are noted parenthetically for guidance.

MRail's patented vertical track deflection system (resource 1) identifies track segments at high risk of failure by comparing loaded and unloaded track deflection. The company buys and retrofits freight cars with the patented system pre-installed (resource 2). The company sells these to freight companies (transaction 1). Freight rail operators use the data collected to maintain track integrity (value 1) and avoid costly derailment events (value 2).

While this narrative covers the key areas, it does so by focusing entirely on the innovation and the process. Our goal is to significantly improve this narrative.

Narrative coherence

Brilliant business model narratives are *coherent.* When something is coherent, it makes intuitive sense because all of the elements fit together as part of the whole. Coherence does *not* require perfect alignment. We all are familiar with imperfect systems that still function effectively: families, schools, governments and (of course) organisations. Coherence just requires that the configuration of elements makes sense and small changes in the configuration would not improve its functioning.

Two other key issues should be considered: relevance and credibility.

- *Narrative relevance.* Does the business model narrative relate directly to the underlying problems and values of the stakeholders?
- *Narrative credibility.* Is the business model linked to credible sources and information? There are many scams and bad actors out there and they can and do use business models purely for their own profit. But smart, ethical investors and partners can reveal whether business models are credible with a relatively minimal amount of investigation. For those of us who strive to build ventures that generate profit and contribute to a better world, credibility is an increasingly important component of the business model narrative.

To see brief examples of these and why they are important, take a look at the Narrative Relevance and Credibility Excursion on the website.

Compelling business models align the narrative and the firm

A compelling business model narrative can be a powerful tool. Some have become so powerful they become *generic.* 'Uber' has become a generic narrative term for disintermediating a service. Just as Uber links drivers with people who need rides, Grappl tried to be the 'Uber for tutors' by linking college tutors with college students who needed a little extra help. HopSkipDrive hopes to be 'Uber for kids', Maidac strives to be 'Uber for housecleaning', FoodConnect fights hunger by claiming to be 'Uber of Food', and so on.

Keep in mind, however, that the characteristics that make a business model easy to communicate are not necessarily tied to its viability.

A compelling narrative is still only a narrative. It is just a collection of words that tells a story. It must be aligned with the actual business model elements. Like organisational culture, it may or may not reflect what actually happens at the firm day to day. As the Grappl example showed, narratives do not always transfer well from one industry or market to another. Further, popular media narratives for big successes and failures are written after the fact. For example, Apple (and Steve Jobs, of course) has become synonymous with product innovation. In reality, Apple's business model innovations emphasized design, usability, software and content access, rather than hardware innovation. For example: Apple did not invent or launch the first MP3 player, the first tablet computer, the first smartphone or the first smartwatch.

Entrepreneurs commonly rely on analogy and metaphor to communicate their innovations, ideas and business models. Analogy and metaphor are powerful narrative tools. They can also be deceptive – hiding real complexity and poorly aligned business model elements behind a story that is convincing and compelling. 'Uber for tutoring' (Grappl) was *too* easy to communicate. The entrepreneur used the analogy to convince himself and a business partner that it was a scalable system. That only prolonged the process of realising that the analogy was flawed.

There are three ways to align narrative with the actual business model. You can change the narrative to fit the elements, change the elements to fit the narrative or you can change everything.

Consider MRail again.

Look back at the narrative we generated a few pages ago. It seems to be coherent. After all, the freight operators are used to dealing with railroad cars. This was just one more car they could incorporate into their operations.

But the freight operators do not want *more freight cars*. They just want to know which track segments are at risk. They did not have the resources to support this type of operation. The freight companies would need to hire engineers with sophisticated laser experience to maintain the physical systems, as well as data and software engineers to review, manage and report the data. And MRail did not want to be in the business of acquiring and retrofitting freight cars for the long term.

This was a case where both the elements and the narrative needed to be changed. There were two critical disconnects in the business model that were revealed by the narrative. First, this was a high-tech company using lasers to make extremely accurate measurements. But the value it would provide to customers (rail operators) was the *analysis* of that data. A key resource in this narrative was rail cars – 20,000 kg of steel that would have to be acquired, transported and retrofitted. The business of buying and selling used rail cars was not an attractive activity! Second, the transaction with customers was also clearly at odds with the business model. The rail companies did not particularly want to purchase more rail cars – they wanted data about track condition. This would be somewhat equivalent to selling a car owner an entire petrol station rather than just the petrol!

In this case, the solution involved changing the key business model elements, the nature of the value created and how it was all connected.

In the first iteration, the plan retained the rail cars but did not require operators to purchase them. The company would generate early revenues by convincing rail operators to allow company-owned cars with the laser measuring system to be towed along on freight runs. The transaction still required a significant operational component, but at least the customers were not paying for the rail cars.

The real solution was to miniaturise the measurement system so that it did not require a separate rail car. This corrected both the resource and the transaction element issues in the narrative. Here is the updated version, which Farritor developed.

MRail helps freight rail operators maintain track integrity (value 1) and avoid costly derailment events (value 2). MRail's patented vertical track deflection system (resource 1) identifies track segments at high risk of failure by comparing loaded and unloaded track deflection. The company's proprietary database of longitudinal measurements (resource 2) generates a prioritised set of track segments based on failure risk. MRail partners with rail operators (transaction 1) to analyse track. The company provides a subscription service (transaction 2) that prioritises track segments for visual inspection. MRail's service reduces visual inspection costs (value 3) and the risk of derailment.

This was the business model that Farritor utilised to develop the opportunity. And, once it became clear that there was a viable system generating valuable data, MRail was sold to Harsco, a global rail services business.

If you would like to see a much more dramatic and complex example of changing business model narrative, please take a look at the Modelling Coherence at CDI Excursion at the website. That tells the detailed story of Cellular Dynamics, one of the world's most innovative companies, going through one of the most fascinating changes in business model narrative we have seen. Once the narrative was aligned with the rest of the business model, the company raised $100 million in private financing, floated on a public stock market in 2013 and was acquired by Fuji for $270 million in 2015. Business model narratives that make sense make a difference.

RECAP

- Great business models align the organisational narrative with the resource, transaction and value structures.
- Compelling business model narratives are coherent, relevant and credible.
- A compelling business model narrative has to make sense to make a difference.

These two business models that Ferguson utilized to develop the [illegible] to become [illegible] a [illegible] and everything [illegible] was able to [illegible] a global [illegible].

If you would like to see [illegible] significant [illegible] example of [illegible] business [illegible] please [illegible] at the [illegible] at the [illegible] website. [illegible] storytelling [illegible] one of the world's [illegible] companies [illegible] one of the most [illegible] business [illegible] two years [illegible] in the business [illegible] company raised [illegible] million [illegible] stock market in [illegible] for $270 million in 20[illegible]. [illegible]

[illegible]

[illegible]

[illegible]

Part 3

The right business model at the right time

'There are an infinite number of business models. Every company is different. Even companies that do similar things in the same industry operate differently.'

Tom Whitaker, Partner, Propel Venture Partners (personal interview)

Take a deep breath. You are halfway through the book and have come a long way. You have all the theory and foundational knowledge you need build great business models.

There may never be perfect agreement on how many unique business models there really are, but at least we can agree on processes for evaluating and building them. In Part 3, we examine specific frameworks to help you build winning business models.

Most people assume that any business model framework can be used for any organisation, regardless of its scale and scope. Some analysis is probably better than none, but using the right tool at the right time will make a big difference. Building a business model for an early stage company should be different from changing a business model for an established, mature organisation. There should be different levels of detail and analysis for different stages of the organisation.

In each of the following chapters, we explore a framework appropriate for organisations at specific stages: pre-venturing, early stage organisations, growth firms and mature organisations. The underlying elements and analyses we explored in Parts 1 and 2 remain relevant for all firms. Too much detail and analysis for an early venture is probably wasted effort. Too little detail and analysis for a growth or mature business probably means you missed something.

You could self-identify the stage of the organisation you want to analyse and skip straight to that chapter. Savvy entrepreneurs and managers, however, will appreciate knowing the frameworks and activities for all stages. After all, there are no hard-and-fast rules to consistently distinguish between the stages. Further, the odds are good that you will revisit these analyses when your organisation progresses to the next phase or when you need to analyse a different organisation!

Once you have these frameworks in your toolkit, you will be ready for Part 4, which discusses more advanced applications of business models, including business model innovation and sustainable business models.

9 RTVN for pre-venture opportunities

'What I tell founders is not to sweat the business model too much at first. The most important task at first is to build something people want. If you don't do that, it won't matter how clever your business model is.'

Paul Graham (co-founder of Viaweb and Y Combinator)

Business model analysis is used at organisations of every size and shape. But the business model really came into its own in the world of early stage venturing. Would-be entrepreneurs wanted an effective tool for explaining their vision. Financiers wanted a better framework than a business plan for evaluating risks and resource requirements.

At the very early stage, however, it is possible to do a lot of well-intentioned but useless analysis. The Lean Canvas and Osterwalder's Business Model Canvas are powerful tools, but pre-launch and very early stage ventures may get the most benefit from the simplest business model framework: RTVN.

RTVN stands for resource, transaction, value and narrative. This framework utilises the most simple configuration of business model components. It is efficient and effective when entrepreneurs are exploring the underlying opportunity.

It is all about the opportunity

Entrepreneurship is all about opportunities. Opportunities are about *situations and information*. Entrepreneurs use information to envision new ways to connect and combine resources and transactions. In the right situation, that new combination will create new value. The entrepreneur and the opportunity are two sides of the same coin.

At this stage, using the wrong business model framework may be detrimental. Why? The more sophisticated frameworks and tools ask questions that the entrepreneur may not be able to answer. Answering those questions might require information that is inaccessible or non-existent. Worse, the framework might encourage the entrepreneur to accept or even invent unproven hypotheses to 'complete' the analysis. The more complex frameworks may mislead an entrepreneur to create or assume structures or elements that seem to fit the overall story but cannot be implemented.

At the pre-venture stage, entrepreneurs should start with the RTVN model.

The RTVN business model design

'In a start-up, it is a race to traction before you run out of money. Hopefully, you are not wasting your precious time on old-style business plans, but many have simply replaced their business plan with a Business Model Canvas or Lean Canvas. While I vastly prefer the Lean Canvas to antiquated business plans, I'm seeing many start-ups falling into the same trap. They start focusing way too early on their business model, especially what their various sources of revenue will be, what their sales channels will be, and what their costs will be, and they leave the pesky matter of "the solution" – can they

actually solve the target customer's problem by discovering a solution that is valuable, usable and feasible – as a (largely coding) task for later. Yet, unless you can succeed in creating real value with your solution, the rest of the canvas won't be worth much.'

Marty Cagan, Silicon Valley Product Group

The RTVN business model design is a simple diagram identifying the key resources, transactions and values in the proposed business model. It helps the entrepreneur tie those elements together with a coherent narrative. It minimises the connections that need to be assessed and focuses on the key elements and overall story of the business model.

At the pre-venture stage, using the more complex frameworks is likely to be time consuming or even misleading. Start simple. The RTVN model is all you need if you are just starting to explore an opportunity.

The RTVN model is shown in Figure 9.1.

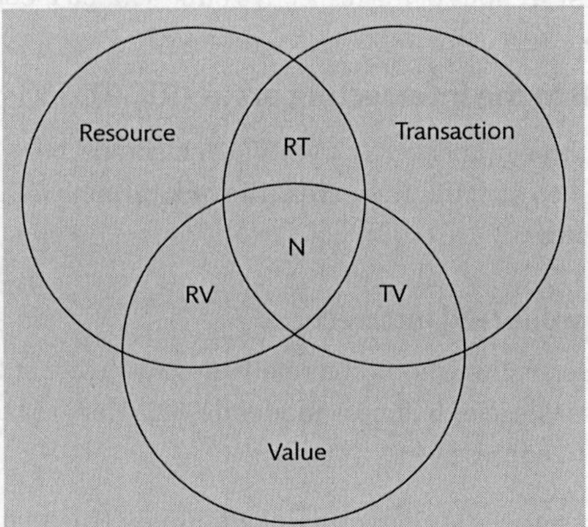

FIGURE 9.1 The RTVN business model for pre-ventures

Worksheet 9.1

THE RTVN MODEL

You can also find the RTVN model in Worksheet 9.1, which you can download from the book website.

Using the RTVN model involves three steps:

1. Identifying the key resources, transactions and value (RTV).
2. Exploring the intersections (RT, TV, RV).
3. Developing and testing the narrative.

Step 1: fill in the main section of each circle (resource, transaction, value)

If you have worked through Chapters 4–8, then this step should be straightforward. You can simply add in your SHaRP resources, the key transactions from your transaction map and your critical tangible and intangible values. Those can be written in the largest sections of the respective circles in the model.

Step 2: fill in the intersecting areas (RV, RT, TV)

There are three of these: RT, TV, RV. Each should be addressed in a specific way. We will walk through all three sections below.

Resource value (RV) intersection

The RV intersection should be relatively clear even at the very earliest stage of business model design. Here are the questions to address:

- Which resources are directly linked to the value that customers need?
- How, when and why do customers need the value that these resources generate?

The RV intersection area emphasises that your opportunity incorporates resources that really can generate new value for customers. If you have identified SHaRP resources in Chapter 5 and you have clear and compelling data from customers about unmet needs, then this section should confirm how those are connected.

If the key issue you are facing in business model design is linking your resources to value creation, there are additional resources that you might find helpful. One good resource is Strategyzer's Value Proposition Design framework. It explicitly walks through the process of connecting the unique resources of your (imagined) venture to the needs or gains that will be valuable to your customers.

> **Video resource**
>
> Watch this short video by Strategyzer explaining the Value Proposition Design framework. It is a very efficient way to work on the RV intersection in your business model.

Just be careful. The danger for most entrepreneurs is that the 'obviousness' of the RV connection prevents the entrepreneur from testing assumptions. There is a resource and there is a value, so they must be connected! The logic for finding opportunities usually follows one of the following two processes:

- *Problem-solving logic* → I see a problem. Specifically, I see potential customers who are experiencing an unaddressed pain or missing out on an unrealised gain. I have developed an innovation that will address that pain or provide the gain. Since it is better than what customers have currently, they are guaranteed to buy it.
- *Resource-extending logic* → I have novel or under-utilised resources (assets, capabilities, skills, knowledge, innovation). I have searched around and found at least one customer

segment that would benefit from those resources. Since they do not use that resource currently, they are guaranteed to buy it.

If you found yourself saying: 'The value to customers is obvious', then you should take a careful look at Resource-Value connections. At the very least, talk to potential customers to confirm or reject basic assumptions about value creation.

Resource transaction (RT) intersection

Although it is not always clearly addressed by entrepreneurs, the RT area is usually straightforward. Review these questions and put summary information into that section of the model:

- Is there a specific sales and/or marketing channel that you will use?
- What resources will be required to establish those channels?
- How will you link your key resources to your primary transactions?

The RT area is often a fact check. You may have the answers to these questions at the very earliest stages of business model development. If you cannot answer these questions or there appear to be significant gaps between your key resources and transactions, this is a great opportunity to step back and think about the business model narrative. Does the business model really make sense? Without RT congruence, the business model has no likely starting point.

Transaction value (TV) intersection

The TV intersection is the most commonly missed in the RTV model. Why? It is probably the least intuitive of the three intersection areas.

Success with customers is about much more than simply creating a better product and making it available. Entrepreneurs tend to underestimate the inherent challenge of ensuring that the transactions fit the value creation process.

Here are the questions to ask about the TV intersection:

- Do customers have unusual or complex transaction requirements? What are those requirements?
- Are customers beholden to other entities or organisations for their use of the target products or services?
- Do customers tend to avoid adopting new products or services from start-up companies?

If the answers to any of these questions are yes, then the TV intersection requires more careful analysis. It is the reason that many entrepreneurs fall into 'build a better mousetrap' thinking.

Think back to the Orbel hand sanitiser story. There was a clear need – improved hand sanitisation for healthcare workers to avoid in-facility infections. Adam Sutcliffe, the product inventor, created a better mousetrap – a product that clearly solved the problem by exploiting the 'bad behaviour' of wiping one's hands on clothing.

The company he formed has experienced some success. He hired a CEO who established international partnerships with distributors. The product won a variety of design awards and generated positive popular media press.

Unfortunately, six years after the original design work, the product has not generated significant revenues or returns to the team or investors. The problem seems to be the TV intersection. The team was strong on retail and promotion, but less experienced with healthcare operations and supply chains. Purchasing by healthcare facilities in most Western countries is extremely complex, often tightly regulated and based on deep organisational relationships. Neither the doctors and nurses who need hand sanitation solutions, nor the patients who benefit from sanitation practices, are directly responsible for product purchasing decisions in clinics and hospitals. In the healthcare industry, the intersection of transactions and value is extremely important.

Because organisations have unusual responsibilities to their customers (patients) and complex reporting requirements (to insurance companies and government organisations), buyers prefer to work with established companies and to rely on previously demonstrated products. It appears Orbel did not establish the transactive structures and processes to address this particular aspect of customer value creation.

Step 3: fill in the narrative (N)

If you worked through the narrative development in Chapter 8, you may be able to come up with some simple phrases or sentences to complete the RTVN framework.

Then it is time to step back and look at the business model as a whole. Do all the parts work together? Does the narrative link all the elements together?

The power of the RTVN framework comes from its simplicity. But with simplicity is the risk that the analysis is based on one or two incorrect assumptions. An RTVN analysis based entirely on innovation and intuition is untested. This is one of the best opportunities to leverage your business model team. Share your analysis with them; ask them to help identify untested assumptions and potential flaws or gaps. This is not the time for secrecy or reticence! Get your first business model in front of smart, experienced and knowledgeable people!

Separating the business model from the innovation

Sometimes, entrepreneurs confuse the innovation with the business model. Keeping them distinct can be difficult when looking into the future to design and build an organisation.

Entrepreneurs and managers are most likely to substitute one for the other when there is no organisation or when a new product or service has not yet launched. There is limited context to evaluate the business itself; it is deceptively easy to use business model analysis tools to evaluate the *innovation, product or service* rather than the *business*.

The innovation is not the business model! It is easy to unintentionally substitute one for the other when the product or service is not yet launched. Remember, you cannot do business model analysis on an innovation! You must focus on the opportunity and the business.

Any innovation can be incorporated into many possible business models. Sometimes, there may only be a few possible business models; sometimes there could be dozens or hundreds! If your analysis focuses on the innovation itself, then you have probably missed other key elements of the business model. In that case, you are not analysing a business model, you are evaluating an innovation opportunity.

In other words, if you try to use business model analysis on an innovation, product or service, you are examining whether the innovation could be successful in the marketplace, not the viability of the business model. These may sound similar and one might lead you to the other, but they are not equivalent.

Think back to MRail. Is there an opportunity for an automated system that uses high-precision laser-based measurements to predict rail track failure? Is there a business model to create a viable company to realise that opportunity? These are not the same question and they do not have the same answer. Some colleagues and I reviewed the opportunity with the inventor, Professor Shane Farritor. The opportunity was moderately attractive: a small market but not a lot of innovation to compete with. The real question was the business model: could we link the key resources to transactions that would work for the customers? You might be interested to know that evaluating the opportunity took us about three months, but figuring out a viable business model took only a couple of weeks. You can read more about the difference between the MRail opportunity and business model in the Opportunity V. Business Model at MRail Excursion at the book website.

Keeping it simple

In this chapter we are focused on RTVN, the simplest business model framework. Business model complexity may not be captured in this framework.

You may be better served with one of the more complex frameworks if any of the following are true:

- You have already developed the opportunity in more depth, including operational planning;
- You have initiated some organisational activities; or
- Your analysis requires more sophistication because of the complexity of the technology, resources or transactional processes.

Before you rush off to take on a greater challenge, make sure you are doing so for the right reasons. Do not do more business model analysis than you have to! Adding more complexity to the framework or analysis will not make the business model better.

There are two key reasons to keep the business model analysis as simple as possible. If the simplest analysis, such as RTVN, clearly shows that the model does not work, a more complex analysis almost always will produce the same result. Only very unusual business models require extremely complex analysis to reveal viability. More complex frameworks usually identify *more* potential problems in business models.

Second, business model analysis using more complex frameworks tends to raise detailed questions about processes and activities. Often, these questions need to be answered through brief experiments or direct engagement with market participants. Whilst such activities are very valuable in any entrepreneurial situation, they can also be extremely time- and resource-intensive. These types of investigations usually should be initiated *after* preliminary conclusions have been reached about the business model. Otherwise, the business model analysis risks becoming an ever-expanding series of questions about the underlying opportunity. These will need to be addressed, but only after you are comfortable with the core viability of the model.

The RTVN framework is a very simple, but very effective mechanism to generate and evaluate the business model for a start-up idea, innovation or new product/service. If you are an entrepreneur looking to launch a new venture or a manager planning to launch a new product or service, this is a very good starting point. Use the worksheet, explore the business model elements and connections and then share the business model with a trusted colleague. Together, you should brainstorm ways to improve the business model with alternative elements or different connections between those elements. You should also look for missing elements, business model connections that do not fit the overall narrative and other inconsistencies or problems.

RECAP

- The RTVN business model framework is a great starting point for pre-ventures and very early stage ventures without a lot of existing infrastructure or activities.
- Start simple: building more complex business models too early may be a significant waste of time.
- Most entrepreneurs and managers are comfortable with the resource–value connection; the most common mistakes are in the value–transaction connection.

10 The Lean Canvas for start-ups

'It's extremely hard to build a company with a product that everyone loves, is free and has no business model, and then to innovate a business model. I did that with Kazaa, had half a billion downloads but that wasn't a sustainable business.'

Niklas Zennström (quoted in 'Skype Founder Wants Startups to Show Him the Money', Bloomberg Online, 30 September 2012

Many entrepreneurs and new business owners do not think about a business model at all. They see a problem, often from their own experience. They find or create a solution. They sell that solution to people and organisations with the same problem. You can read about an entertaining example of this, the Squatty Potty, in Squatty Potty Excursion on the book website.

Some business launches, however, would benefit from business model analysis. Kazaa was a good example of solving a problem whilst lacking a business model. Kazaa's peer-to-peer network never developed a clear mechanism to monetize traffic, even after it settled numerous copyright lawsuits and sorted out spyware issues.

Business model analysis has begun to replace business plan writing as the standard process for exploring new venture viability in many schools of business. See the Business Model or Business Plan Excursion at the book website for more about this.

Whilst the RTVN framework is sufficient for business model analysis at the idea stage, it lacks the specificity and operational detail needed for more complex and non-obvious opportunities. The Lean Canvas is a great framework for evaluating business models that have gone beyond the ideation stage.

A lean approach to entrepreneurship and business model design

The Lean Canvas incorporates Eric Ries' Lean Startup' framework. You can read more about that in the Lean Startup Excursion, including a summary of Lean Startup principles.

The Lean Startup emphasises an *experimental* approach to entrepreneurship. Rather than plan for every contingency or strive for the perfect product, Lean Startup thinking requires getting ideas and solutions to customers as soon as feasible. In other words, the arbiter of product viability is the market, not the entrepreneur.

In this context, *a business model is part of the experiment.* Any given business model should be seen as a hypothesis rather than a certainty.

The Lean Canvas

The Lean Canvas tool was created by Ash Maurya as an adaptation of Osterwalder's Business Model Canvas. As Maurya notes, the key purpose is to 'capture business model hypotheses on a single page'. The Lean Canvas is shown in Figure 10.1.

The Lean Canvas prioritises experimentation over detailed planning. Use the Lean Canvas to identify some of the key market entry experiments that will test your business model. Emphasis is equally divided between the customer, the innovation/opportunity and the organisation that will exploit the opportunity.

Please note: four of the elements in the Lean Canvas are the same as in Osterwalder's Business Model Canvas: channels,

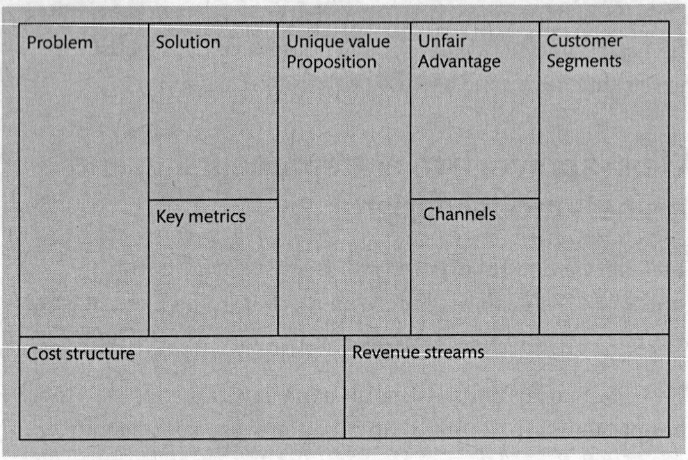

FIGURE 10.1 Ash Maurya's Lean Canvas

Source: adapted from https://blog.leanstack.com/why-lean-canvas-vs-business-model-canvas-af62c0f250f0; Lean canvas is adapted from The Business Model Canvas (http://www.businessmodelgeneration.com) and is licensed under the Creative Commons Attribution-Share Alike 3.0 Un-ported License

customer segments, revenues and costs. We will discuss those here. In Chapter 11, we will only mention them so as not to be repetitive.

Building a Lean Canvas: the e-parking opportunity

Using an example can clarify how to use a canvas like this.

Many US and UK university campuses do not have enough parking for all faculty, students, staff and guests. Is there an opportunity here? Adam spent a couple of idle hours coming up with some ideas, eventually settling on an online market-making platform. We will explore the Lean Canvas business model in the context of this opportunity. 'Adam's e-parking business (AEB)' Lean Canvas can be accessed online.

There are many websites offering tools for business models and business model canvasses. Adam used www.canvanizer.com, which you can learn more about in the Canvanizer Excursion at the book's website.

We will look at each area of the Lean Canvas. We will start with the elements closely related to the resources from the RTV framework: problems, solutions and key metrics. On the online AEB, the business model resource elements are shown as red sticky notes.

Lean Canvas element 1: problems

The 'problems' in the Lean Canvas are the *customers' problems.* Business models exploit an opportunity associated with an unmet need. In other words, if you have not identified a customer problem, whether it is a pain or an unrealised gain, you have no business model.

The Lean Canvas is especially helpful for new entrepreneurs and very early stage ventures. It makes the customer problem explicit.

Consider the AEB Lean Canvas. There is not enough parking. Actually, that is the *situation,* not the *problem.* It does not describe a pain or unrealised gain. So we need to dig deeper.

The lack of parking causes problems for two customer groups. People who want to park on campus but cannot experience numerous possible pains. They may have to walk or find alternative transportation; both could create a time penalty. They might have to pay more for parking elsewhere or alternative transportation, which are financial burdens. The institution may have complex administrative arrangements to determine who is eligible for parking on campus. That creates a financial burden or an opportunity cost – someone is being paid to spend time on this instead of more valuable activities. The institution probably deals with some number of ongoing complaints about parking, especially as the student body turns over regularly. This could generate HR costs as well as longer-term costs associated with negative perceptions about the institution.

The obvious solution, new car parks, is extremely costly and requires extensive space. The institution might be lacking one or both of these resources.

Can you think of any other problems? Remember, any problem should be clear, specific and quantifiable.

Lean Canvas element 2: solutions

Right next to the problems are the proposed solutions. Again, clarity is important here. A 'solution' is not a product or service. It is whatever needs to be utilised in order to address specific aspects of the problem.

At the top level, the 'a–ha' moment for this problem was the simple reality that the majority of colleges and universities are located in cities where nearby residents have driveways (or possibly even garages) that are unused during working hours. In other words, it may be useful to reframe the problem. There is enough parking in the area, but the university doesn't actually own it.

Just identifying the solution, of course, does not solve the problem. The real solution requires figuring out the rest of the business model, starting with the specific solution elements. The first step is realising that the owner of the property has to have the right to set pricing and access limitations. The second step is recognising that the commuters (students, faculty, staff, guests, etc.) need to be able to select from available options.

Once these intermediate steps have been clarified, the idea of a crowd-based market for parking seemed worth exploring. In years gone by, the information system needed to operate such a market might have involved a physical bulletin board, a folder in a file cabinet managed by the campus grounds team, or perhaps even some sort of spreadsheet maintained by a diligent administrator. Today, of course, we have dramatically better options, including any web or mobile applications. A website where property owners could list their 'space', including availability and pricing, would then be easily searchable by the users, who could reserve a space for a day, a week, a month, a semester, a year, or perhaps even longer.

It should be evident that this solution has the *potential* to address the full set of problems in the canvas. As we will see in the 'costs' section, one of the most attractive aspects of this solution is that it replaces the cost of a traditional *physical* car park with the cost of a *virtual information exchange.* This links perfectly to the fact that the problem was not the lack of space, but the lack of information about available spaces.

If you are already getting excited about this idea, remember to be wary of solutions that seem too good to be true. We believe entrepreneurs should test boundaries whilst recognising real legal and ethical constraints.

'Napster was predicating its business model on violation of copyright.'

Dan Farmer

Can you think of any other key elements of the solution? Perhaps a novel form of payment? Perhaps some type of feedback or rating system so that users get more complete information about options? What if the owner misrepresents how large or accessible the space is? What if the user leaves her vehicle beyond the agreed time? What if the user tells a friend who parks a different car there, whether at the right or wrong time?

Lean Canvas element 3: key metrics

Key metrics are the data measures that will determine whether the opportunity is viable as well as whether the organisation is exploiting the opportunity effectively. Key metrics are the quantification of critical success factors (CSFs). If the entrepreneur or organisation gets these wrong or cannot implement them effectively, the venture has very little chance of success.

For more about the special challenges of key metrics, please see the Key Metrics Excursion on the book website.

Let us look at AEB again. What are the key metrics for whether this is viable for a given institution? We suspect that the current cost of parking on or near campus will be at the top of the list. Our anecdotal investigations of student complaining about on-campus parking often reveals that the costs are often not that onerous. Students simply would prefer to spend their money on other goods. Some of the indignation appears to stem from the belief that parking should be included in tuition. Another metric will be the quantification of faculty/staff parking needs. This is, arguably, the more stable, longer-term customer population (students are, all else equal, somewhat transient customers); property owners might be more comfortable with faculty/staff than student customers. Arguably, however, one of the most important metrics will be the acquisition (and maintenance) cost associated with obtaining access to driveway space. If the cost (in time and money) is too high, the pricing model will limit the number of customers willing and able to buy parking. Similarly, the cost of maintaining and updating the system, including relevant information, has to be modest enough to allow the market to generate reasonable profits. Once the system is up and running, another key metric will be customer (especially student) turnover rates.

What are the key metrics for your opportunity? How will you measure them?

Try to identify the four to five critical success factors (CSFs) for your opportunity, the key metrics associated with those CSFs, and how you would collect the data to evaluate the metrics. This is also a great time to think about any industry or market experts that you could contact to discuss CSFs and key metrics.

> **Worksheet 10.1**
>
> **CRITICAL SUCCESS FACTORS**
>
> Download this worksheet from the website. Use the worksheet to explore CSFs and key assumptions in your business. The worksheet encourages you to identify those people and the assumptions you would ask them to confirm or reject.

What are the key metrics for your opportunity? How will you measure them?

It is time to move on to the transaction dimension of the Lean Canvas. That includes customers, channels and revenue streams. This should feel familiar to the RTV analysis from Chapter 9. On the AEB canvas, the elements for transactions are shown in blue.

Lean Canvas element 4: customer segments

Customer segments are simply groups of customers that share the same needs or purchasing preferences. Let us think about the AEB example again. Many people want parking on a college campus: students, faculty, visitors. But they do not have the same buying criteria. For example, it is likely that a visitor unfamiliar with the campus will be willing to pay a higher fee for a few hours of parking for convenience. A student who will need to get to campus every day is much more likely to investigate transportation alternatives to avoid paying that daily convenience cost. A member of the college faculty might be willing to pay more than the student, but might also consider longer-term options such as buying or renting a home based, in part, on transportation alternatives.

It should be immediately obvious that 'visitors' are not a good target market for the AEB, unless the parking problem is truly severe. There is a time and information cost to using the system – a visitor would probably prefer to pay a little more rather than sign up for the system.

The AEB elements hint at the likely purchasing preferences of the three segments. These are based primarily on my own anecdotal observations and comments from my students. Good business model canvas analysis, even at this early stage, should include data. Data would answer the following questions, as a starting point:

- What percentage of students are willing to walk an extra mile to save 10 per cent on parking?
- What percentage of students would need parking access after normal hours? Until midnight? All night?
- What percentage of faculty and staff get parking on campus? How much do they pay?

For many more resources about customer segments, please see the Customer Segment Excursion.

Worksheet 10.2

CUSTOMER SEGMENTS

Download this worksheet from the website to explore customer segments and purchasing preferences. You may not have the necessary data to develop definitive customer segments, but it is definitely worth your time to write down your assumptions. This is often one of the most powerful activities in our entrepreneurship courses. Students sometimes have very naive assumptions about how customers purchase products or services and why potential customers behave differently from each other. Identifying your hypotheses about customer characteristics and purchasing preferences will go a long way towards clarifying what research you really need to conduct about customers. After all, the Lean Canvas is specifically intended to help you make your assumptions explicit so you can test them.

Lean Canvas element 5: channels

Channels are simply the paths to reach customers. To complete this section of the canvas, you want to answer the following questions:

- How will you and your organisation inform potential customers about your product/service?
- How will customers purchase and pay?
- How will you deliver products/services to customers?
- How will you provide post-sale support?

A customer journey map can be a powerful tool for thinking about channels and other aspects of engaging with customers. Read more about this tool in the Customer Journey Map Excursion on the book website.

If you have already identified and investigated reasonably well-justified customer segments, it is very likely that you will discover that different customer segments require different channels. For the AEB, we would use different channels to appeal to students versus faculty. Further, because the AEB is a market-maker, the property owners can also be thought of as customers (or, alternatively, suppliers). A campus email might get to students and faculty, but property owners will need some sort of direct selling effort to convince them to participate. That might be phone calls, a letter delivered to the mailbox, or even going door-to-door for personal conversations. All customers ultimately will use the web or mobile app as the transaction channel, but an educational channel is required to start the process.

Many students and would-be entrepreneurs fall into the social media trap. They fiat the marketing plan, stating: 'We'll use social media', with no further analysis or details. As anyone who actually works in social media or has run a social media campaign can tell you, it just is not that simple. To read more about this challenge, check out the Social Media Marketing Trap Excursion.

Lean Canvas element 6: unfair advantage

The 'unfair advantage' element in the Lean Canvas often causes angst amongst new entrepreneurs. Students in my classes commonly report unfair advantages that are unsustainable or simply mistaken, such as 'great app design' or 'quality marketing'. After some questioning and discussion, many students (and entrepreneurs) discover, to their horror, that they cannot clearly identify an unfair advantage.

This is normal.

Here is Maurya's comment about this element:

'I was cognizant of the fact that few startups have a true unfair advantage on day one which means this box would be blank . . . This box wasn't intended to discourage you from moving forward on your vision but rather to continually encourage you to work towards finding/building your unfair advantage. Once a startup achieves some level of initial success, it is inevitable that competitors and copy-cats will enter the market. If you don't have a defense against them, you stand a real risk of being made extinct by these fast-followers.'

An 'unfair advantage' is something that competitors cannot easily copy, acquire or otherwise execute. Structural unfair advantages can be generated by:

- unique and protectable intellectual property (such as a patent);

- individuals who simply know more about a specific topic through years of study and experience;
- economies of scale in production or other processes that generate virtuous cycles of benefits (such as cost savings);
- unique and protectable relationships with other organisations, such as a long-term contract with a key supplier, partner or customer; and
- unique and proprietary information (e.g. trade secrets) such as confidential information about customer needs.

You might be interested to note that whilst the AEB might not have an unfair advantage at the start, it could build a structural (and potentially sustainable) unfair advantage. The AEB leverages a scarce resource: empty driveway spaces. If the organisation commercialising the AEB idea can get property owners to sign long-term (e.g. three years/ five years) agreements, it would be effectively impossible for another company to compete. This type of advantage is called supplier (or customer) lock-in. It is a little unusual, but it does happen.

Another possible form of structural advantage would be if the AEB online market becomes generally acknowledged as the 'standard' platform for a given campus. That might happen if the organisation were able to get some sort of formal (or informal) agreement with the institution to promote or otherwise legitimise the platform. This type of platform standardisation happens in many contexts. For example, eBay because the dominant online auction site is in the USA, the UK and other markets. eBay's dominant position is self-feeding. Buyers want to use a platform that has the most sellers; sellers want to use a platform that has the most buyers. It is difficult to compete with organisations that have created *de facto* standards, precisely because there is an explicit cost for customers to choose not to use that standard.

You have used the Lean Canvas to more carefully explore the resource and transaction dimensions of your opportunity. It is time to unpack the value dimension. There are three elements to guide the analysis: unique value proposition, costs and revenue streams. On the AEB canvas online, these areas are shown with yellow notes. Once you complete these, we can discuss testing assumptions and you will be ready to build great business models for start-ups.

Lean Canvas element 7: unique value proposition

The heart of the Lean Canvas is the unique value proposition (UVP). Ash Maurya describes this element as: 'A single, clear, compelling message that states why you are different' and worth potential customers' attention.

You might be asking, 'If Maurya means for it to be so simple, why is it one of the biggest spaces on the canvas? And why does Adam have no fewer than five different statements on it in the AEB?' Great questions!

The ultimate goal in the Lean Canvas is to get to a single compelling value proposition that customers will pay for. A key purpose of the Lean Canvas, and 'lean start-up' thinking in general, is to generate hypotheses and make assumptions apparent. If your business is early stage enough to warrant using the Lean Canvas, then there is probably still some uncertainty about your unique value proposition. Your short-term goal is to create experiments that will help test and evolve a minimum viable product.

The AEB has not, to our knowledge, ever been implemented. Adam has brought it to the attention of transportation administrators at multiple universities. We can safely state, however, that it remains unclear whether it would actually work or what scale would be needed to make it cost effective. Adam has 'tested' the idea with a limited number of students, faculty and even homeowners; the results were quite inconclusive. The general concept makes sense to people (especially students), but property owners have been hesitant about the idea of letting students, or anyone else, park in their driveways. Two big unknowns are legal liability and insurance costs for the venture.

We have left five possible 'unique value propositions' in the AEB because that is the stage of the opportunity. They all seem possible to us; some are interconnected. The business model has not been progressed beyond this stage – critical data is still missing and critical assumptions remain untested. We suspect that some of these possible UVPs could turn out to be the final key components of a minimum viable product.

The customer journey model you created is one of the best starting points for thinking about UVP. What needs and/or pains bring the customer to the transaction? Under what conditions will they decide to make the purchase, rather than go without, stick with what they already have or choose a competitor or substitute option?

Sometimes, UVPs seem so obvious that entrepreneurs do not bother to test them. This is unfortunate because testing UVPs can be quick and easy. To learn how to do it, read the Unfair Advantage Excursion.

Lean Canvas element 8: costs

No value analysis is complete without addressing costs. Depending on how early you are in your business model analysis, you may have little or no definitive cost information. But that just means this is the right time to start collecting it.

For simplicity of discussion, the AEB shows only launch costs. A full analysis should include estimates for running operational costs. It is always important to prioritise your efforts. More information about prioritising cost research can be found in the Prioritising Cost Research Excursion at the book website.

Starting the AEB venture would include some research costs: identifying and canvassing the portfolio of properties within a given area. Someone is literally going to have to walk around to all those properties and identify the ones that should be targeted as having an available space. Then some number (50?) of those property owners need to be contacted to try to get them to agree, in principle, to the idea.

The next critical cost is developing the online marketplace for parking spaces. There are resources online to help provide rough estimates for creating web and mobile applications. Entrepreneurs should be comfortable using such resources with caution; my experience is that these estimators are commonly off by a factor of three or four times. An estimator might suggest $50,000 for an alpha launch, but the reality could be as low as $10,000 or as high as $250,000. Better data would be an estimate from an actual app development group or by scoping out hiring the developers needed on contract.

It is not possible to address all cost types with the same level of detail. Some costs will be easily identifiable; others will require detailed research, thoughtful estimation or intuition-based guesswork. Create an estimate using the best information you have. If you have no information, get some! Search the web, call business connections, create a quantitative model to incorporate some of the underlying factors. Do what you can to put some boundaries around the likely cost structure. Ultimately, your costs estimate needs to inform your overall business model viability analysis. Most of the time, a reasonably good estimate will get you there.

Lean Canvas element 9: revenue streams

Every entrepreneur's favourite part of the business model canvas is 'revenue streams'. This is, after all, where the magic happens.

When we discuss OBMC in Chapter 11, we will distinguish more carefully different types of revenue and pricing mechanisms. For now, we just want to make sure that you have methodically considered a reasonable variety of revenue mechanisms tightly linked to your customer needs and value proposition.

To understand why revenue streams are often not as simple as we like, please read the Hammers and Revenue Streams Excursion at the book website.

Consider the AEB. No one wants to buy a car-shaped piece of land on campus. It is more accurate to state that what they want is somewhere to put a car in reasonable proximity to their on-campus activities. Once that distinction is made, it opens up the opportunity to a variety of alternative solutions, including novel revenue mechanisms. The AEB focuses on creating a marketplace for driveway space near campus. The obvious option is charging a fee on each marketplace transaction. But will that generate enough revenue? Can we come up with something more inventive? You can read about a variety of interesting possibilities in the AEB Revenue Stream Excursion.

We hope this gives you some food for thought about your own opportunities. Very often, entrepreneurs latch onto the first revenue stream they identify and never explore alternatives. If you have not considered alternatives, we strongly encourage you to brainstorm some new ideas. The odds are reasonably good that you will return to your original revenue stream. Even if that is the case, you might develop some new insight about your customers or ways to generate revenue.

Testing assumptions

If you have done the work in this chapter, you should have the key information to populate a Lean Canvas. If you created a canvas on Canvanizer, you may already be finished!

Before we move on to the OBMC for established and growth ventures, let us reinforce one of the most important benefits of the Lean Canvas and Lean Startup framework. At this stage of development, entrepreneurs should be focused on surfacing and testing assumptions. The purpose is to create quick, inexpensive 'experiments' that drive towards a minimum viable product: something that can be sold to actual customers to address the original opportunity.

In the case of the AEB, a minimum viable product might include only a student worker, a spreadsheet, some sort of co-insurance arrangement with the college and a basic contract for both the property owner and the person who needs a space. Or it might just involve a survey of local homeowners to see if any would be willing to learn more about it.

The Lean Canvas is a powerful tool for organising your thoughts, ideas, assumptions and information about your opportunity. It is an excellent tool to test what you know and believe about your entrepreneurial opportunity. Used well, it provides a clear and effective business model map for exploring and testing the short- and long-term viability of a new venture.

RECAP

- The Lean Canvas is an excellent tool for exploring the business model of a nascent or early stage venture.
- The Lean Canvas provides a basis for testing hypotheses about the business model via experimentation and data collection.
- The Canvanizer helps you visualise your core assumptions in the opportunity.

11 The Business Model Canvas for growth

'Money, while clearly helpful in solving myriad problems, can often conceal a business's real flaws. It can also risk rigidifying a company's business model at the very moment it should be in 'customer discovery' mode or iterating around market opportunities.'

Maelle Gavet

Our focus in Chapter 11 is the framework that put business models in the spotlight. Alexander Osterwalder introduced the Business Model Canvas in his book, *Business Model Generation*. Osterwalder's Business Model Canvas (OBMC), shown in Figure 11.1, reflects a practice-focused approach to building business models. It reflects how entrepreneurs use business models as an organisational development and planning tool. The full OBMC can be downloaded from Strategyzer.

The OBMC is a commonly used tool in university entrepreneurship courses. It is a staple of business venturing competitions, accelerators and incubators. It is referenced by entrepreneurs and financiers as a critical part of the business planning and development process.

Whilst the Lean Canvas focuses on the problem statement and opportunity, the OBMC focuses on the venture itself.

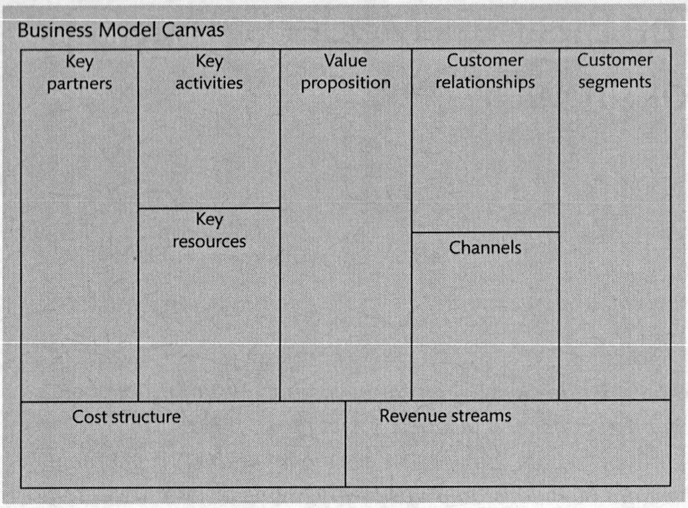

FIGURE 11.1 Osterwalder's Business Model Canvas

Source: adapted from https://strategyzer.com/canvas/business-model-canvas, This work is licensed under the Creative Commons Attribution-Share Alike 3.0 Un-ported License

The OBMC helps to address operational and growth issues in the business model. It provides a flexible framework for thinking about business model adaptation and innovation.

The OBMC

We reviewed the Lean Canvas in detail in Chapter 10. We will therefore explore the OBMC more briefly, focusing primarily on the elements that differ from the Lean Canvas. You should refer back to Chapter 10 to fill in details as needed.

There are nine business model elements in the OBMC. Five are replicated in the Lean Canvas: cost, revenues, value proposition, channels and customer segments. The OBMC uses four elements that were not carried over into the Lean

Canvas: key partners, key activities, key resources and customer relationships.

A great two-minute video introduction to the Business Model Canvas has been created by Osterwalder's consulting firm, Strategyzer. You may also (legally) download the first part (72 pages) of Osterwalder's book, *Business Model Generation.*

We will explore the Canvas via a real example. MRail was an actual company that Adam helped investigate prior to formation. He worked with the founders to develop the venture's business model. A key step was the transition from a product-selling model to an information services model. That investigation took about three months of primary and secondary research on customers, market, operations and financial modelling. The process and results are dramatically simplified in this chapter! MRail's technology ultimately was acquired by Harsco who markets the system through its Protran Technology business.

For illustrative purposes, we have created canvases for both the original product-based business model and the information services business model. Links to the online canvases (OBMCs) for MRail can be found at the book website. It is a good idea to access those now, as we will be referencing them throughout the chapter.

The elements of the OBMC fit very cleanly into the resources, transactions and value dimensions. As we discuss each element, we note some of the key questions and issues. The full, original version of the OBMC has useful questions embedded in it.

Worksheet 11.1

USEFUL QUESTIONS IN THE BUSINESS MODEL CANVAS

Download this worksheet from the website to begin thinking about how your business model addresses these key issues.

Resource dimension: key partners, key resources and key activities

In the OBMC, the resource dimension is clearly linked to partners, resources and costs. Key partners and key resources are not in the Lean Canvas: they replace the 'problems' and 'solutions' elements. In the Lean Canvas, our focus was understanding the nature of the underlying entrepreneurial *opportunity*. The OBMC focuses on how the business model connects the activities and capabilities of the *organisation*.

OBMC element 1: key partners

The OBMC emphasises the importance of partner and collaborator organisations. Who are they and why are they important? How are they connected to the key resources and key activities of the organisation?

Many small and growing firms select partners on a purely opportunistic basis. MRail was a perfect example. The inventor of the MRail technology, Professor Shane Farritor of the University of Nebraska-Lincoln, had been introduced to Union Pacific (UP), headquartered in nearby Omaha. UP provided a used railcar for Professor Farritor to install his first rail deflection system. The company helped coordinate the logistics of hauling that railcar behind coal trains to collect data on major rail lines across the USA. A viable business model required that UP become a paying customer, not a research partner. UP was, in effect, providing free resources to Farritor on a goodwill basis.

It was a great way to bootstrap the idea and get real-world validation of the track quality measurement system, but a partner is very different from a customer. Worse, if the partnership were too close, it could preclude the venture from selling to other customers. The railroad industry has complex dynamics. Competitors often share resources, such as the rail infrastructure, and coordinate activities and information, such as train locations, to avoid disasters such as collisions or derailments. But they are still competitors; it was unclear if a partner like UP would allow MRail to sell services to other railroads.

Who would the right partners be? In the original plan, where the company sold entire rail cars including the track deflection measurement kit, there were no clear partners. MRail would have to do everything itself. A solution focused on data management pointed towards numerous possible partners. That might include: a manufacturing company that could produce self-contained kits installed on any railcar; railcar services companies, including leasing and repairs; rail inspection and services companies; possibly large logistics and equipment companies already embedded in the industry, such as ABB or Siemens.

These types of partnerships are also attractive because they represent potential exit opportunities. The most likely acquirer of a track deflection technology business would be a large firm already in the sector, not a railroad.

OBMC element 2: key resources

Osterwalder recognised the critical nature of the resource-based view of competitive advantage. He saw that a business model was only as good as the resources it utilises to create value. Entrepreneurs have certain resources available and other resources that can be relatively easily obtained. Some resources, however, will pose challenges due to expense or limited access.

The OBMC starts with relatively easy questions. What are the key resources you already use? What resources would increase the value created for customers? As with partners, the real value comes from seeing how this element links to the others.

Let us take a look at the MRail OBMCs. What are the differences in key resources between the original and revised MRail business models? The obvious change is from physical equipment to information systems. With that change comes the need for specific data management and analytical capabilities. The relationship with the railroads is moved into the customer relationships area. Instead of rail stock, a key resource will be the engineering that turns the technology into a smaller 'product' that can be retrofitted onto any railcar. Did MRail have SHaRP resources? Read the MRail Resources Excursion at the website to explore this more carefully.

This is a great time to create your first OBMC using Canvanizer. That's the same website we used for creating Lean Canvases. It's simple and free. You will gain a lot more from this chapter if you start your own OBMC. Doing is far more powerful than just reading. Come up with some type of business idea or begin mapping out your current business. If you do not know where else to begin, start with the key resources.

OBMC element 3: key activities

Key activities are an under-appreciated element of a viable business model. 'Activities' are sometimes confused with either capabilities or even transactions in organisational analysis.

When we talk about activities in business model analysis, we are focused on the activities that are critical to value creation, customer relationships and channel management. The challenge is identifying which activities will make the difference. What puts the '*act*' in *act*ivity?

ACTivities that drive business model viability are Assessable, Critical and Timely.

Assessable activities can be observed, measured and improved. Some entrepreneurs believe they can leverage activities based on capabilities that generate value but cannot be articulated. They are confusing 'tacit' capabilities with 'ambiguous' capabilities. A tacit capability, like riding a bicycle, is learned by experience and practice rather than explicit instructions. An ambiguous activity sounds good until you dig into it, such as: 'We will use world-class coding skills to build apps that people love.' To learn more about the difference between tacit and ambiguous capabilities in the context of key activities, please read the Tacit Capabilities Excursion.

A customer journey map (see Chapter 10) can help you evaluate whether your key activities are *critical* and *timely*. If you skipped Chapter 10, it is worth your time to explore this valuable tool. No matter what your customer journey map looks like, you can use it to generate an activity map for your business model. For each major node, process, event or milestone on your customer journey map, there should be a corresponding *critical* business model activity. There may be overlaps: some activities might be linked to multiple stages of the customer journey map; an event in the customer journey map might be linked to multiple business model activities. The correlation does not need to be one-to-one. But, if you have no activity associated with a given event on the customer journey map, then it is apparently out of your control. That is almost certainly not a good thing!

> **Worksheet 11.2**
>
> **CREATE AN ACTIVITY MAP**
>
> Download this worksheet to use the customer journey map to create your critical activity map.

Finally, key activities are *timely*. This may seem obvious, especially to business people with operational and logistics experience. For new entrepreneurs or managers of growth companies, however, the challenge is recognising that timing is just as important as purpose. Are the activities initiated and completed when needed? Are they operating continuously at the organisation or triggered by specific events? If your key activities are so ambiguous that measuring them would be very time-consuming, expensive or impossible, then you have a problem.

Let us see how all this applies to MRail. In the original product-based OBMC, the key activity was acquiring and retrofitting rail cars with the laser-based track quality measurement system. Working with 20,000 kg rail cars that can only be moved along pre-existing rails is a logistics nightmare. Assessability is straightforward (cost, availability, location), but timeliness presents all sorts of problems. Just getting the railcar to the right place at the right time requires access to a 200,000 kg locomotive engine that is, simply put, already being used by someone else.

In the information services OBMC, the company's primary assets are the data and analytics that provide track quality assessments. Timeliness is no longer a question of railcar accessibility. Now the key activities require efficiently updating the dataset and providing almost real-time information and recommendations to the rail operators. The activities are still assessable: key metrics will be average time between measurements for any given section of track, average system uptime and overall data integrity.

If you completed a Lean Canvas, you should already have some (or all) of the key metrics for your business model; those should be integrated into the key activities in the OBMC.

For more information read the Timely Activities Excursion.

Before we move on to the transaction dimension, think back on the overall resources base of your business model. The biggest differences between the OBMC and the Lean Canvas are in this dimension. If you did not complete a Lean Canvas, you should consider completing the 'problem', 'solution' and 'key metrics' portions. Even though they are not explicitly part of the OBMC, they are extremely useful for thinking about how your resources function within your business model.

Transaction dimension: customer segments, channels and customer relationships

Osterwalder recommends starting the OBMC with the customer segments and customer relationships elements. Using the OBMC assumes that the entrepreneurial opportunity is focused on getting the right innovation to the right customers, not assessing whether the innovation is itself viable.

The customer segments and channels elements in the OBMC are effectively the same as in the Lean Canvas. Rather than reiterate what needs to be addressed for those areas, we will go into slightly more depth for the MRail OBMC.

OBMC element 4: customer segments

It is worth restating that customer segments are simply groups of customers that share the same needs or purchasing preferences. That analysis can be taken forward two steps in the OBMC. First, we want to directly address the importance of the 'Crossing the Chasm' challenge mentioned in Chapter 3. Second, we want to better characterise potential customer segments by size and type.

The key lesson from 'Crossing the Chasm' is that entrepreneurs are often fooled by the behaviour of a small subset of the target market that is enthusiastic about an innovation. These 'technology enthusiasts' actively seek innovations and accept imperfect technologies in order to remain at the leading edge. But they comprise a very small segment of the market. Entrepreneurs misinterpret adoption by technology enthusiasts as proof that their innovation is market-ready. In fact, the vast majority of the market will adopt the innovation only when it has demonstrable economic benefits and established credentials.

To read more about this critical challenge, please see the Crossing the Chasm Excursion on the book website. To read about a specific example where a start-up company could not 'Cross the Chasm', please read the Crossing the Chasm Excursion on the book website.

In addition to understanding segment adoption timing, the OBMC should be used to prioritise customers and segments based on segment size: which segments are the largest and which segments are growing the fastest? You may choose not to target or serve the largest and/or fastest growing segments, but you should certainly do this consciously rather than on autopilot!

Worksheet 11.3

INNOVATION ADOPTION

Download this worksheet to compare what you know about customers to the innovation adoption curve.

For the MRail OBMC, the customer segments are relatively straightforward. MRail could sell directly to railroads or it could sell to rail services businesses. In the USA and the UK, rail companies can be segmented by what they haul (passengers v. freight) and scale of operations (national, regional, local). Rail services businesses can be similarly segmented by scale and by type of services they provide. But it is not immediately obvious which segments will be the most attractive. Is there a difference in customer segmentation between the product model and the information services model? Think carefully, then read the MRail Segments Excursion to learn more.

OBMC element 5: channels

The OBMC explicitly identifies five phases in channels: awareness, evaluation, purchase, delivery, after sales. These should match up to your customer journey map! Based on that map, you should think carefully about your target customers' preferred channels. If you have the time and resources, you could begin exploring channel efficiency. If you have even more time and resources, and are considering multiple channels, think about how those channels work together (synergy) or potentially cannibalise each other (conflict).

The vast majority of companies, especially early stage and growth companies, serve customers through either the company's preferred channel or their competitors' preferred channel. The first should be obvious. When the business was launched, the founders or managers relied on hypotheses about how to reach customers. Those hypotheses might have been well-informed or not. Once in place, however, channel structures tend to become entrenched. There are costs to change your primary channel, not least of which may be re-educating your customers.

What about MRail? Both the product and information services business models probably will require direct sales. There are relatively few customers. The installed solutions might be relatively consistent across customers, but inevitably there is going to be customisation to meet the specific needs of each rail operator's routes and infrastructure.

For many early stage companies, detailed exploration of channel options may exceed the attention and resources available. In-depth channel analysis is also generally beyond the purpose or intent of the OBMC and first-time business model creation. The website for the book provides links to additional resources for exploring channel analysis in more depth.

For a more detailed discussion of channel challenges, as well as some great resources on channel management, please see the Channel Challenges Excursion at the website.

OBMC element 6: customer relationships

The customer relationships section of the OBMC differs significantly from the Lean Canvas. The Lean Canvas focuses on the unfair advantage that the company and/ or innovation will strive to obtain relative to competitors. The OBMC emphasises the customer relationship rather than the innovation. The OBMC recognises that different segments may require different relationships. Note that these relationships are not the same as channels.

Depending on the segments and the channels, customer relationships may range from personal one-to-one connections to completely disintermediated, arms-length interactions. Working with entrepreneurs and students, we found that emphasising two specific characteristics of customer relationships appears to be the most helpful. Those characteristics are proximity and engagement.

Proximity refers to how close or direct the relationship is. In our technologically connected world, however, this might not mean geographical proximity. High proximity relationships require that someone from your organisation be available and connected to the customers at all times.

Engagement refers broadly to the level of interaction and contribution to the relationship. Low engagement relationships require little participation beyond the exchange of goods for value. High engagement relationships require the participants to pay attention, express opinions and contribute to the transaction.

Figure 11.2 shows the different customer relationship types based on proximity and engagement. No quadrant is always inherently better than any other. At the same time, there is likely limited benefit from being stuck in the middle. If engagement is valuable, then increasing engagement should improve customer relationships. Waitrose (UK) grocery stores provide a great example of customer engagement. At the checkout counter, customers receive a token, which they can

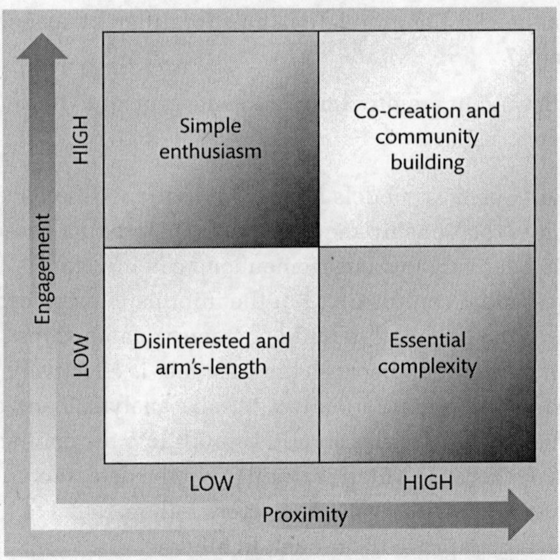

FIGURE 11.2 Engagement and proximity in customer relationships

use to vote for one of several local charities. Each month, the store donates a portion of its profits to the charity selected by its customers. This low-cost system reinforces the customers' sense of community during every visit to the store.

For more discussion about customer relationships, read the Proximity and Engagement Excursion.

If you can identify the proximity and engagement requirements for your customer relationships, you will have great insight on how your business model generates sales. Here are the key questions you will need to answer:

- What are the segments' preferred relationships with the company?
- How do existing relationships integrate with the company's resources and value propositions?
- Are the relationships cost-effective?
- What relationships already exist?
- Do you need different relationships for different customer segments?
- How important are proximity and engagement to those relationships?

The MRail business models revealed important differences in customer relationship requirements. The product-based OBMC is relatively low engagement and can therefore rely on essential complexity. But the information services OBMC has the potential to build customer relationships based on co-creation. Because the customer is effectively purchasing data and information, MRail's analytical and data interpretation capabilities should be built into the contract. In addition, because MRail will still own the data, there is the potential to aggregate data across rail operators to continuously improve the model. In other words, as MRail collects data longitudinally, it should be able to match that data against actual failure and repair information to continuously improve the model's predictive power. That is something that every customer will want.

Value dimension: value propositions, costs and revenues

The OBMC uses the same elements as the Lean Canvas for the value dimension. The OBMC references 'value propositions' rather than 'unique value proposition'. This reinforces the OBMC's focus on the venture rather than the innovation.

Because the frameworks are substantively the same, we will focus on a few questions and details to help explore the elements in more depth, and reference the MRail OBMC to finish the example.

OBMC element 7: value propositions

Establishing the value proposition requires three steps:

- Identifying the pain or gain.
- Demonstrating that the product/service addresses the customer need.
- Linking the value proposition to competitive advantage.

Step 1: identifying the customers' pain or gain

The hard truth is that many entrepreneurs and managers do not fully understand why customers buy from their companies.

If you have already used empathic design principles to observe customer behaviour, then you may have a good understanding of your customers' pains or gains. A 'pain' is an unsolved problem; a 'gain' is a benefit to the value they already have.

In the MRail example, rail operators face two interconnected problems or pains. First, they face enormous costs when faulty track causes a derailment. A derailment is a catastrophic event immensely disproportionate to the apparent cause. The second problem is that visually monitoring thousands of kilometres of track is a logistical impossibility. This leaves the railroads with two unappealing options: accept very high recurring costs for track monitoring or live with high derailment costs.

The bottom line: spend time observing and acting with your (potential) customers to fully understand their needs.

Read the MRail Customer Pain Excursion for more information on this problem.

Step 2: demonstrating that the product/service addresses the customer need

A good starting point is simply listing the features of the product or innovation. What are its characteristics? What are its specifications? What benefits does each key feature confer on the users?

For most ventures, there is no way to do this without interacting with customers. Some entrepreneurs and business managers prefer to develop ideas and launch products and services in relative secrecy. There are circumstances where this type of secrecy is important or necessary, but our experience is that this is not generally a good idea.

Wherever possible, it is important to get the product or service, or some reasonable facsimile, in front of potential customers. The feature you thought was the differentiator might turn out to be either a minimum criteria or even unnecessary. *Only the customer* is the final arbiter of what is a 'must-have' versus a 'nice-to-have' versus a 'no value' feature.

It is essential to develop an explicit list of customer needs and wants. This should have emerged, formally or informally, from your customer journey map and customer observations. Great opportunities are usually characterised by a clear, almost linear, set of connections between the product features and the customer needs.

Step 3: linking the value proposition to competitive advantage

Great business models are only the starting point for building successful businesses. Ultimately, the business model needs to guide the firm towards sustainable competitive advantage. Long-term sustainable competitive advantages separate great companies from merely competent or good companies.

The simplest sustainable advantages come from unique resources, capabilities or structural advantages that competitors cannot easily copy or acquire. Sometimes these are very physical or explicit assets, such as land rights or patents. Sometimes they are tacit or intangible, such as unique design skills or engineering talent. Sometimes they are purely structural, such as economies of scale or long-term contracts. Nearly all such advantages differentiate the company from competitors based on either a better cost position or more effectively meeting customer needs.

Think about these two questions:

- If your product or service provides value to customers by reducing their costs, will you be able to continuously reduce your own costs to stay ahead of competitors?
- If your product or service better meets customer needs, can you charge a premium to pay for further development to stay ahead of competitors?

To support this specific challenge, Osterwalder's Strategyzer group developed a 'Value Proposition Canvas' to complement the OBMC. This can be a very helpful tool to guide your thinking about value proposition.

OBMC element 8: costs

As with the Lean Canvas, it is essential to separate start-up/launch costs from recurring operational costs. Even if you operate a going concern, you should explore and distinguish the one-time costs associated with launching a new product or service.

The OBMC encourages focusing on the most important and the most expensive cost elements of the business model. It is always clever to acknowledge the prevalence of 80/20 rules (e.g. 80 per cent of the costs come from 20 per cent of the system). At the same time, make sure you are aware of whether those expensive items are the ones that actually drive value in the business model.

For more about this, read the Cost Analysis Is Like Checking the Weather Excursion at the book website.

The purpose of identifying costs in the Lean Canvas and OBMC is to guide your thinking about how and why the business model does or does not work. Once you have made a decision to move forward, it is likely that you will want to put together much more sophisticated cost analyses and projections. Use external validation to make sure you have not missed anything important. Industry experts and managers should be able to help you ensure that you are accurately identifying the key cost components.

In the MRail product-based OBMC, acquiring rail cars would represent one of the largest costs of the operation, taking into account cash expense, time and logistics. But the rail cars actually add zero value to the overall system. In the original business model, they were simply a mechanism for enabling the measurement equipment to travel with the train.

OBMC element 9: revenues

The Lean Canvas focuses on what customers will actually buy. The OBMC explores alternate and optimal revenue mechanisms.

Start with your value propositions. What is it that customers really need and what will they pay for?

Worksheet 11.4

REVENUE ALTERNATIVES

Download the worksheet to explore a simple matrix of revenue alternatives. Brainstorm as many different revenue mechanisms as you can based on the types described in the table.

Once you are clear about what the customer will pay for, consider alternative revenue mechanism types. Try to distinguish the specific nature of the product/service based on whether you sell, rent, subsidise or license something to the customer. Does the transaction happen only once or is it recurring? What are the advantages or problems for using that mechanism type?

What did MRail's customers really want to buy? Surely not railcars! And they did not really want laser-based track deflection equipment. And, when you get right down to it, they did not want a large-scale database of rail quality for their entire track system. They just wanted to know which short segments of track were most likely to fail and required immediate visual inspection.

Great work! You should have now built at least one, and possibly two or more, business models. If you used all three frameworks (RTV, Lean Canvas, OBMC), then you have a toolkit designed to help you generate brilliant business models at any stage of venture development.

RECAP

- The OBMC provides a more thorough analysis of the business model for an early stage or growth venture.
- The OBMC is most powerful in ensuring that your business model effectively connects the resources and capabilities of your venture to specific customer segments with clearly identified needs.
- Use the OBMC to explore alternatives: new revenue models, new channels, new customer segments, new value propositions.
- The OBMC is most effective when you recognise that some information is relatively easy to obtain or confirm; use the 80/20 rule to your advantage.

12

Beyond basic business models

'[T]he implementation of multiple business models is not a risk but rather a new tool for strategists.'

Casadesus-Masanell and Tarziján

The business model entered mainstream management via technology entrepreneurship. Most of this book has focused on entrepreneurial contexts. But *every* organisation has a business model that can be identified, evaluated and adapted.

In this chapter, we look at business model analysis in the context of 'big' business. We can use the same tools, but we must address the increasing levels of complexity that arise with larger entities. That may require more sophisticated business models or the use of multiple business models.

Going beyond basic business models

Identifying and assessing business models for large, complex organisations requires some careful thought about the purpose of the analysis. A high-level analysis using the OBMC, for example, may be sufficient to explore emerging challenges in competitive positioning or new flaws in the value proposition–customer segment connection. This type of analysis often can be done relatively quickly without over-focusing on detailed operational issues.

If, however, senior managers believe that the threat to the organisational business model is significant and ongoing, the high level analysis may not provide sufficient detail to explore alternatives.

In our classes, students prompted to identify the business model for a large corporation tend to default to variants of the company's logo, slogan or most recent advertising scheme. Apple's business model is described as 'cool products for creative people'; the business model for Walmart/ASDA is 'low prices for everyday products'. These are not business models; they are pithy and memorable catchphrases that capture what these organisations want consumers to remember.

Business model analysis is powerful precisely because it summarises extensive information into simple narratives that can be conveniently analysed and assessed. This strength, however, can become a significant weakness when the underlying information is too complex for effective simplification. Apple, for example, derives extensive revenue and profit from a variety of related but distinct products and services including the App Store, iPhones, desktop computers, laptops, tablets and iTunes music sales. Simplifying this to a few sentences will miss many of the key characteristics and capabilities that have propelled Apple to its status as the most valuable company in the world.

Business model analysis for large, complex organisations requires one of three processes – each with benefits and drawbacks. When brevity and simplicity are valuable, the analysis can use of any of the frameworks we have explored. These analyses are quick and efficient, providing a high-level perspective on the organisation's key strengths and challenges. This is best used as a filtering tool to identify areas for further exploration.

The second option is to explore a focused a business model in much more depth, expanding the various business model elements into their own analyses. We discussed the RTVN, Lean Canvas and OBMC tools in Chapters 9–11. Using one of these tools with data collection and careful thought provides a detailed examination of a complex business model. This will diagnose a business model that appears to be failing as as well operational changes and innovations available. The analysis might still be summarised in a single page canvas, but that summary is unlikely to truly reflect the more subtle and noteworthy issues revealed in the analysis. Complex business models cannot always be represented in a simple canvas.

Finally, there is the option to address multiple business models. For some organisations, this is the only realistic option, especially during troubleshooting and (re)design. Explicitly accepting that an organisation has multiple business models often simplifies the analytical process because each product–segment connection can be explored effectively without interference from other company activities. The key to valuable analysis, however, will be tying the business models back together.

Analysing a complex business model is relatively straightforward; it requires more attention to detail and depth for each business model element. Tackling multiple business models is a different story, because multiple business models in the same organisation may be parallel, connected or synergistic.

Complex business models

The OBMC is an excellent tool for exploring the business model of larger organisations. Because it focuses on organisational elements and processes, rather than the opportunity, it can be expanded to address large, complex organisations.

For example, the Strategyzer's Value Proposition Design canvas expands the link between the 'value proposition' element and 'customer segment' elements in the OBMC. This provides a simple way to explore multiple customer segments and multiple product/service offerings.

As organisations become larger and more complex, they can either focus on scaling up their core business model or explore other business models.

Analysing the business model for a large organisation may therefore be as straightforward as deconstructing each of the major business model elements using the various tools and worksheets provided in this book. In general, we recommend using the OBMC rather than the Lean Canvas, because it focuses on the organisation rather than a specific opportunity or innovation. Table 12.1 shows how each element of the OBMC can be explored using the various business analysis tools and frameworks we have already discussed.

In effect, mapping a complex business model differs only in scope. Use the full set of tools at your disposal, summarise effectively and keep in mind both the forest and the trees.

As a straightforward example, consider a grocery store. Most grocery stores use one business model to serve multiple product segments: families with small children, health-conscious athletes, budget-minded customers, and so on. The store might offer convenience products, organic foods and low-price staples including store branded foods.

The resources, activities, channels and other elements of the main grocery business model are mostly or entirely consistent with these value proposition–segment pairs. It would be possible to walk through the full set of elements, using the underlying frameworks identified in Table 12.1, and populate a sophisticated OBMC.

Business model analysis is, therefore, appropriate, but not uniquely needed for this type of situation. There are a variety of marketing, sales and channel-oriented tools and frameworks to address product–channel–customer fit.

At the same time, business model analysis can be valuable for exploring alternatives and novel approaches to otherwise familiar examples.

Most grocery stores sell cooking staples such as oil, vinegar, spices and liquors. But shopping at most grocery stores is

TABLE 12.1 Using the OBMC to explore complex business models

Business model dimension	Business model element	Research and data collection frameworks
Resources	Key resources	SHaRP analysis
	Key activities	Customer journey map
	Key partners	RT and TV analyses
Transactions	Customer segments	Value proposition design; Crossing the Chasm
	Channels	Customer journey map: awareness, evaluation, purchase, delivery, after sales
	Customer relationships	Proximity and engagement analysis
Value	Value proposition	Value proposition design
	Cost structure	Launch and operating analysis: 80/20 rule
	Revenues	Brainstorming alternative revenue mechanisms

a heavily routinised process that has been optimised for efficiency and throughput, given the relatively low markup in the industry.

Trends such as the slow food movement and changing lifestyle preferences have created opportunities for alternative product–channel–customer combinations. For example, Germany's rapidly growing venture Hello Fresh delivers weekly recipes and fresh ingredients straight to your doorstep, so you can cook delicious, quick and healthy meals at home. Similarly, the UK's Graze customises your snacks using a refined data analytics engine to deliver weekly requirements through the post. A standard grocery store would struggle to completely change the 'grocery shopping' experience to accommodate some of these trends. It would require changes to other parts of the business model that would make the model incoherent and inefficient.

Instead, entirely new businesses have arrived to offer very different food experiences. Speciality stores like Demijohn in Edinburgh and larger chains like Vom Fass have capitalised on these trends with different business models. They sell speciality and small batch runs of liquors, oils and other foods and drinks at dramatically higher prices than generally found in grocery stores. Customers are expected to come to the store to try one or more samples, to linger and chat with the servers. Both the products and the experience represent a completely different approach to selling food 'staples'. Exploring the business models of these types of organisations would reveal key differences in cost and revenue structures, key activities and other areas.

In the USA, most grocery stores have stayed focused on the core grocery business model. Most of these can be evaluated effectively within the context of 'complex business models'.

The largest grocery organisations in the UK, including Tesco and Sainsbury's, have expanded dramatically from food and food-related products to financial services, clothing and mobile phone contracts. We could still use the 'complex business model' approach, but it is almost certainly more useful to think of these as parallel or connected business models.

Parallel business models

'But reinventing and pioneering new business models is both exciting, potentially very financially rewarding, and perhaps even more importantly, easily accessible for entrepreneurs starting from scratch.'

Diane Osgood, business innovation director at Virgin

Operating parallel business models is not a new idea. Any holding company with disparate business entities is, effectively, operating parallel business models. Some large organisations really do run completely different businesses – Richard Branson's Virgin arguably being a very good example. Some of Virgin's operating businesses are partly or tightly connected. Virgin manages a number of related businesses in transportation, for example. On the other hand, links between the transportation, healthcare and media businesses are not obvious. Branson's argument has focused consistently on taking risks, accepting failure and winning by being good at running businesses, rather than any unique or industry-specific capability.

For Branson, the value of parallel business models was ensuring that no single entity became unmanageably large. Diagnosing a business model problem is fundamentally simpler in smaller organisations.

'In our record companies, when the business got slightly too big, I would get the deputy managing director and the deputy sales manager and the deputy marketing manager and say, "You are now the managing director, sales manager

and marketing manager of a new company . . . " We'd split the company in two, and then when that company got to a certain size, I'd do the same thing again.'

Richard Branson

Parallel business models within organisations have become somewhat rare. The popularity of using distinct business models within a larger organisation has waxed and waned. In the 1970s and 1980s, corporate strategists used the BCG growth–share matrix to show how different business models could be used to balance cash flow across multiple entities. But this has fallen out of favour. Corporate strategy has moved to a more competency-based framework for creating competitive advantage. Sophisticated financial products and markets have reduced the benefits of using one business to subsidise another.

If your organisation is operating parallel business models, you can simply analyse each one independently using any of the frameworks we have explored. Parallel business models have no significant connections or interactions; changes in one business model, including shutting it down, should have no substantive impact on the others.

If you are operating parallel business models, it is reasonable to make sure that doing so makes sense within a single organisation. Virgin appears to be the exception that proves the rule; the company is as unique as its entrepreneurial founder.

Connected business models

'What surprises me [about management teams that are simultaneously operating multiple business models] is that the differences between the business model metrics, tradeoffs, scale and competency requirements have not been made explicit . . . One of the models tends to dominate with the balance delivering moderate or even unprofitable performance.

Keith Mackenzie

Tesco, the UK-based grocery store, has dramatically expanded into a variety of other services and industries. Is the company operating one large business model, multiple parallel business models or multiple connected business models?

This is a challenging question. Good arguments could be made for each option. Perhaps Tesco's business model can be described as a one-stop, low-price shop for almost every common consumer product and service. Perhaps the grocery, financial and technology services are really parallel models that just happen to be exploited in a common retail facility. Or perhaps the commonality across customer needs and the use of infrastructure point towards business models that are distinct but connected.

Connected business models operate within a larger organisation but share elements across the business model dimensions. A great example of this is W.L. Gore. Most consumers recognise the company's Gore-Tex® fabric used to make waterproof clothing and shoes. But the underlying technology supports materials used in fields ranging from medical devices to heavy manufacturing and even cell phones.

To develop, produce and sell products across such distinct fields, Gore uses a variety of organisational processes that differ across the business model elements. The biopharma customer segment differs significantly from the shoe manufacturer segment. The transactions and value propositions differ as well. Arguing that these all fit within one very complicated business model is likely counterproductive; the differences within each element would require very detailed and confusing contingencies.

On the other hand, the different business models are clearly connected by very specific organisational resources and capabilities. Two stand out for special consideration. First, Gore is a globally recognised leader in a very specific area of materials, 'expanded polytetrafluoroethylene'. This technology forms the basis of nearly every Gore product and technology solution.

The second combines a truly atypical culture with unusual organisational structuring. Gore emphasises a merit-based, innovation-focused culture. It has been written about extensively; we can note a few key points. First, every employee is an 'Associate'. Hierarchy is relevant only when associates make commitments to follow others on specific projects and activities. Second, the company takes a truly long-term approach to innovation and employee development. The company ensures that product development activities occur in close proximity to other functions such as marketing and customer support. Finally, Gore does not allow facilities to grow beyond a certain scale – usually 150–200 people. When a division, group or facility exceeds this limit, the company splits and/or relocates groups to ensure that there is a high degree of familiarity and communication within each facility.

Connected business models can be powerful drivers of opportunity. Gore is regularly recognised for its innovation outcomes. It is one of only 12 companies to have been on Fortune's '100 Best Companies to Work For' every year.

Google (okay, 'Alphabet') provides another, more complex example of connected business models. Alphabet's core business generates online advertising revenue (via Adsense and Admob). But it is predicated on the value of big data – perhaps the largest owned dataset in the world. That data is immensely valuable for directing and monetising advertising activity, but Alphabet is obviously putting it towards other uses. The list of Alphabet owned and funded ventures is constantly growing, but a few clearly show how the company's expertise in data extends beyond advertising.

The concept of self-driving automobiles is driven entirely by data acquisition and analysis. The sensors and software on a self-driving car must acquire and analyse an incredible amount of data in real-time. Now, imagine that a centralised machine learning system uses all of that data to continuously update its own algorithms and decision rules. The real power of a system like Waymo is not that Alphabet has great programmers and data management tools. It is that the central system can integrate and learn from *every car using the system.*

A human driver hopefully learns from her driving experience. She might drive anywhere from a few thousand km to 20,000 km in a year. But if Waymo has 50 cars operating, each driving 10,000 km/year, then the system is learning from 500,000 km of experience each year. And the benefit of that experience is automatically available to every vehicle. In 2016, Alphabet announced that the system had accumulated 2 million miles of experience. In addition, it was resimulating *3 millions miles of driving each day.*

The underlying resources of data acquisition, management, analysis and machine learning that power Google's original search engine technology are being employed to everything from self-driving cars to biotechnology, weather prediction, home energy use, robotics and more abstract concepts such as geopolitical security and artificial intelligence.

Working with connected business models requires explicit recognition of those connections, especially when the analysis focuses on business model change and innovation. Whilst analysis can begin with the elements that are connected across models, we recommend that managers treat the models as parallel to fully uncover connected elements. Starting with the separate models also tends to reveal how many different models are actually required.

Gore, for example, has 10 different product categories. Business model analysis could evaluate each category separately. The connection across categories is, however, relatively straightforward: a common chemical/material and a highly idiosyncratic organisational culture and structure. If you were to use business model analysis on Gore, you might want to evaluate those first within the resources dimension and then populate separate canvases based on product–customer segment pairings.

Alphabet, on the other hand, would require complex and sophisticated business model analysis intended to cover the entire organisation. Beyond the sheer number of variety of business models in play at Alphabet, some are more than connected. Google uses its knowledge of web content to generate advertising revenue (Adsense), but it also uses the promise of advertising revenue to generate content (YouTube). These types of business models are self-reinforcing – they are synergistic.

Synergistic business models

'[W]e predict that most leading technology companies will have five or more business models . . .'

Accenture: Scaling to Succeed in New Business Models

There are no inherent advantages to multiple business models. In fact, venture capitalists and private investors are notoriously wary of start-up companies attempting to implement more than one business model at a time. Different business models have different risk/reward profiles and different capital requirements. The one thing they all have in common is the requirement for managerial attention, usually the resource in shortest supply.

But some innovations and organisations can benefit from multiple business models that generate synergies. Some, in fact, are viable only because of those synergies.

In the case of Google and YouTube, the synergies we can see now are straightforward. It is worth keeping in mind, however, that Google was roundly criticised when it acquired YouTube in 2006 for $1.65 billion.

Some examples are less obvious but more clearly demonstrate how synergistic business models may be at the core of an organisation's viability.

Return Path is the global leader in email marketing intelligence and deliverability.

The company states on its website: 'We partner with more than 70 providers of mailbox and security solutions, covering 2.5 billion inboxes—approximately 70 percent of the worldwide total.' Through its partnerships with ISPs, consumer networks, clients and dataset aggregators, Return Path also utilises data from more than 2 million individual consumers and more than 5000 retailers. The combination of these various datasets gives Return Path unique insights into the 'how' and 'why' of email marketing, enabling the company to set standards that distinguish good practice from spam.

At the heart of all these statistics are a couple of basic realities about our increasingly digital lives:

- People and organisations rely on email.
- The majority of email is spam.
- The difference between spam and real email is not always obvious.

Return Path relies on two synergistic business models to resolve this challenge. They refer to these as the 'sender side' and the 'receiver side'.

The receiver side business model requires partnerships with major ISPs and email providers (e.g. Comcast, Microsoft, Yahoo!, Orange, TimeWarner, Yandex, etc.) to collect and integrate data on email deliverability outcomes. In other words – which emails go to the inbox v. the junk/spam folders, and why? Return Path's data from more than 2.5 billion valid inboxes gives it unique insight into email outcomes.

The relationships in the receiver side business model, however, do not generate significant revenues for Return Path. Return Path collects and integrates the inbox data to generate data about mail deliverability. The company returns the integrated data to those partners to help them improve their internal filters and systems. Return Path also uses this data to help the industry set standards for email marketing practice and to reduce the threat of phishing and other email-based crime.

It is the sender side business model where this is monetised. Return Path leverages its expertise with email deliverability to provide software and services to email marketers that want to ensure that valid email marketing campaigns get through to the customers who want them.

Figure 12.1 shows this visually. This is a different 'map' from the business model canvases that we have used so far, but you can see the simplified key resources, transactions and values.

The reality is that neither of Return Path's business models works without the other. The receiver side business model

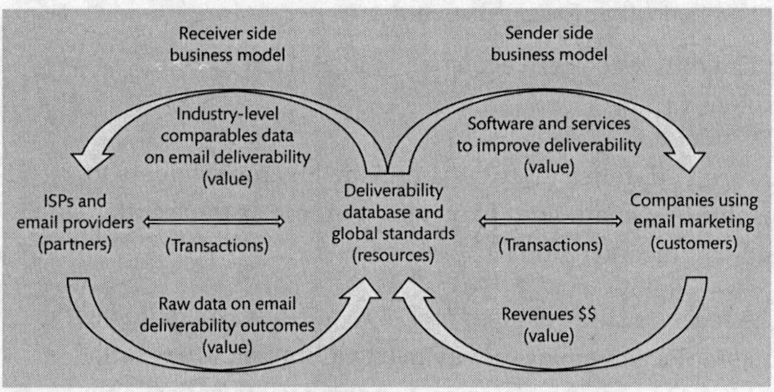

FIGURE 12.1 Return Path's synergistic business models

is, for all practical purposes, a not-for-profit model that generates high-level knowledge about problematic email outcomes. It is possible that ISPs and email providers would pay to have the integrated information, but sharing it with them makes it much easier to convince them to provide their inbox data in the first place. On the sender side, the global database establishes the company as the most qualified expert in the world. Without that, the company is just one more email marketing services business.

Return Path could be shown with a third cycle associated with global non-profit organisations associated with email and information security, including Signal Spam, the Online Trust Alliance, the Anti-Phishing Working Group and DMARC.org (Domain-based Message Authentication, Reporting and Conformance). But we thought the diagram was complex enough already, especially if you are not an email marketing expert.

Synergistic business models incorporate at least two such interlocking cycles of resource, transaction and value structures. One of the challenges with developing maps for synergistic business models is finding the right level of detail. Even simple variants of such synergistic maps may be confusing to people who are unfamiliar with the RTV framework. After all, each of the cycles shown in Figure 12.1 could be shown as a full RTV diagram or business model canvas.

Building truly synergistic business models is neither simple nor easy. In the case of Google and YouTube, it is not clear whether Google fully anticipated the synergy or simply recognised that online video was going to be an enormous asset. Former Google CEO Eric Schmidt once stated that Google paid $1 billion more than YouTube was worth, even as analysts recognised the synergistic potential of users uploading content and being exposed to paid advertising.

Similarly, Return Path's journey to the synergistic business model took more than a decade, including multiple acquisitions and divestitures. Return Path executives believed that email would be the 'killer app' for a long time; proven access to email users was clearly valuable. In a way, the key resource in the business model might have been something else entirely: the belief that the company could be the 'good guy' in the email space finding highly innovative ways to eliminate spam and fraud.

There is a not-so-subtle irony in the Return Path business model story.

Return Path was predicated on the challenge of ensuring that email users received the promotional emails they wanted, whilst unwanted or fraudulent email was filtered to the spam folder. The president of Return Path once told us that spam filtering by focusing on trigger words ('V!agR@') was, effectively, 'a losing arms race with the bad hats out there'. Changing spam campaigns is a near-zero-cost process; addressing the fallout from successful phishing attacks can be very expensive.

So Return Path changed the entire premise. Rather than filter out (blacklist) everything that looked bad, why not certify (whitelist) senders that live up to a set of approved email marketing standards. Some of those standards can be quite complex, but a simple example is just including a one-step, validated 'unsubscribe' feature.

The sender side business model, where Return Path actually makes money, is therefore predicated on ensuring that promotional emails get to the inbox. But when we describe this in our entrepreneurship classes, students often interpret this as resulting in more spam!

The bottom line is that synergistic business models can be incredibly powerful. At the same time, they can be difficult to describe, much less design and implement.

RECAP

- Larger, complex businesses also have complex, multiple business models that can co-exist and be synergistic.
- Whilst parallel business models can exist, it is becoming increasingly rare and businesses often prefer connected models instead.
- Connected business models operate within a larger organisation but share elements across the RTV business model dimensions.
- Some businesses can be synergistic business models, where the individual models somehow are able to reinforce each other to create and capture value.

Part 4

Business model innovation

'Talking about "our business model" is a pleasant diversion. It was the diversion of the dot.com era, the fodder for venture capitalist pitches and the endless source of conversation – and speculation – at social gatherings around the globe. Everyone was drawing models on napkins, and no one was executing. It's the fun part of business, but in reality it's the most serious of all the matters before us. Creating it and implementing it successfully is real work.'

Faisal Hoque, CEO of BTM Corporation

In the final part of this book, we will go beyond building great business models.

A key lesson from this book is that business models are not static. Truly great business models must adjust to changes in the organisation, the market and the industry. In this section of the book, we'll introduce the business model cycle, which provides a simple framework for continuously evaluating and updating your business model over time.

One of the most exciting recent developments in business strategy is the concept of business model innovation (BMI).

Numerous large-scale studies suggest that BMI has become an important driver of industry change and exceptional organisational growth. In Chapter 14, we will explore the drivers of BMI and the factors that determine whether BMI succeeds or fails.

In Chapter 15, we will explore the idea of sustainable business models. 'Sustainability' is a word with multiple meanings; nowhere are business models more confusing than in the context of sustainable organisations. Some business models can be sustained over time; some business models strive to be environmentally sustainable. There is no direct connection between the two, at least for the foreseeable future.

Finally, we will close the book in Chapter 16 by returning to business model basics. There are important, simple lessons to remember, regardless of the sophistication of your analysis or the brilliance of your business model idea. The tools and frameworks in this book are most useful when they complement the hard realities of business models in the real world.

13 The business model cycle

'Newspapers with declining circulations can complain all they want about their readers and even say they have no taste. But you will still go out of business over time. A newspaper is not a public trust – it has a business model that either works or it doesn't.'

Marc Andreessen

Business model creation and analysis might appear to be a one-time, linear activity.

The 'business model' we construct on paper is, at best, an approximation of what is actually desired or happening at the organisation. But 'The map is not the territory.'

To paraphrase Reid Hoffman, the founder of LinkedIn, you need to live your business model in permanent beta. The business model that you capture on paper, whether RTV, Lean Canvas, OBMC or a combination of models, should be treated as a running hypothesis that is constantly tested and questioned.

Business models benefit from planning, research and careful analysis. There is a time for brainstorming, intuition, logic, data collection, analysis and revision. Ultimately, however, a business model is an *experiment.* It is a design of organisational resources and activities intended to create value for stakeholders, including customers, users, partners, employees and owners. But the outcome of the experiment will not be certain until it is implemented and measured.

The business model cycle provides a framework for designing and testing business models.

The business model cycle

As we discussed in Chapter 1, business model designs need to be tested, specific metrics identified and recorded. The business model cycle (BMC) is a simple, four-step process for building and testing business models (Figure 13.1). The four steps of the BMC are: troubleshoot, (re)design, test and (re)deploy. Although the BMC can be started at any stage, most managers and entrepreneurs will find the 'troubleshoot' stage the most intuitive place to begin. If you are building your business model from scratch, then you are implicitly beginning at (re)design.

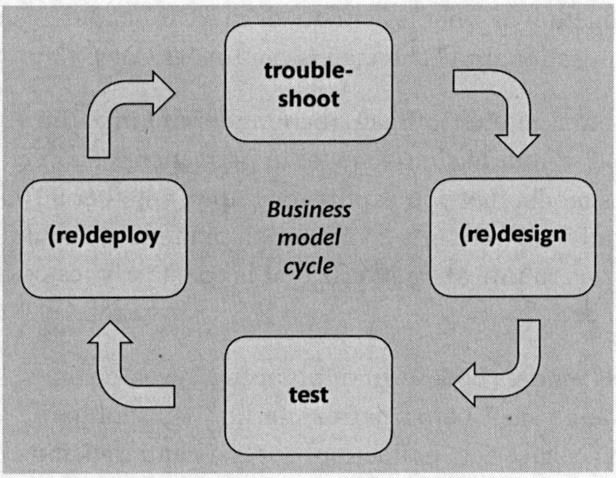

FIGURE 13.1 The business model cycle

Troubleshoot

If you have followed the guidance in this book and built at least one completely new business model, you effectively started the BMC from the (re)design stage.

Most business model analysis starts with troubleshooting. A manager or entrepreneur recognises that some aspect of the business is not running properly. Revenues and/or profits are down, customer satisfaction is sliding and employee engagement has peaked. Whatever worked before is not working now.

Adjusting or innovating the organisation's business model should not, however, generally be the first step. Troubleshooting should start with a series of questions to confirm whether the business model is the right tool for the job.

First, is there a simpler solution than business model change? Table 13.1 shows the four types of organisational symptoms most commonly mistaken for business model failure. It also provides the questions to ask about those symptoms and the factors that distinguish business model failure from other organisational problems.

The four symptoms most often mistaken for business model failure are: falling market share, low working capital, suboptimal product/market fit, slow market uptake and high operational costs. Review Table 13.1 to learn which questions to ask.

When there are one or two key operational failures, such as operating inefficiency or poor product-market fit, it is generally best to assume that the business model is *not* the problem. Why? Because changing or innovating your

TABLE 13.1 Is it the business model or is it something else?

Symptom	Key questions	Alternative explanation to business model failure
Falling market share	Are competitors behaving differently? Have customer needs changed?	Poor competitive strategy or strategy implementation. Poor product/market fit.
Low working capital	Are changes in the cash conversion cycle linked to specific operational changes? Are working capital deficiencies linked to supply or inventory levels?	Poor cash management. Poor growth or inventory turn management.
Slow market uptake	Is the target market segment attractive? Is there a clear plan for crossing Moore's chasm and advancing from the core segment to other segments?	Poor evaluation of market and overall opportunity. Product/service features specific to early adopters rather than mass market.
High operational costs	Have operational efficiencies kept up with changing market/industry conditions?	Inefficient production or resource utilisation.

business model is a relatively high-risk proposition. We will discuss this in depth in Chapter 14.

If, however, there are numerous operational failures or the symptoms go beyond these causes, then the business model becomes the next most likely suspect.

Similarly, if you have identified opportunities that require more change than incremental product improvements or entering close market segments, a new business model may be needed.

TABLE 13.2 You probably need a new business model when . . .

Problems	▌Operational failures cannot be attributed to only one or two core causes. ▌Market adoption problems do not seem to be tied to operational issues at all. ▌Industry conditions are changing faster than you can adjust operations.
Opportunities	▌New products or services require more than incremental changes. ▌You believe that current products or services could be attractive to markets that are significantly different from the markets you currently serve.

Table 13.2 shows the types of troubleshooting results that suggest that it is time to implement the business model cycle.

The best troubleshooting step is to complete one of the business model canvases (RTV, Lean Canvas, OBMC) based on your current business. Where in the business model are the problems? If the problems can be isolated to only one or two specific elements in only one or two areas, then you should start with an incremental approach to change. If the problems are more systemic and/or if they link multiple factors across multiple business model areas, then the odds are good that a (re)design is required.

'In any business that grows big on one business model, transitions can throw everything in the air.'
Bing Gordon, general partner and chief product officer at Kleiner Perkins, former chief creative officer at Electronic Arts

(Re)design

If you have been following along and doing the worksheets, you have already been doing business model (re)design. (Re)design is, generally, the most interesting and entertaining part of the business model cycle. In short, business model redesign explores new business models by removing various constraints or assumptions. For example, (re)design could focus on alternative configurations of the current business model elements, it could incorporate entirely new elements or even eliminate some elements.

Broadly speaking, the sky is the limit! We will discuss why the best (re)design efforts take nothing for granted. Business model (re)design should brainstorm exotic and apparently unlikely options.

The RTVN and canvases can be used during (re)design. One of the reasons we encourage the use of the online Canvanizer tool is precisely because it encourages rapid and wide-ranging exploration. If you have built a canvas, you can simply copy it (so you do not lose your original) and then begin experimenting. They are especially helpful when you are working with an existing business model. The canvases encourage you to reconfigure the business model in non-intuitive ways.

Some entrepreneurs (re)design simply by drawing new business model configurations or processes. This can be especially helpful when there is no existing business model to build from. These often start with mind maps centred on either the apparent problem or the proposed solution.

During the (re)design stage, the key questions you must answer are:

1. Does the proposed business model create and capture sufficient value to warrant forming or changing the organisation?
2. Do the elements of the proposed business model work together in a coherent system?

3 Does the proposed business model appear to be stable and sustainable?

(Re)design is most effective when entrepreneurs surrender the core assumptions they have about the possible business model. The MRail (re)design was an excellent example. The underlying assumption was that customers (rail operators) wanted to own the rail quality measurement system in the form of a retrofitted rail car. Once the team recognised that all the rail operators wanted was the data to prioritise visual track inspections, the (re)design progressed relatively smoothly.

For another good story of (re)design, read the Recurve Excursion at the book website.

In the (re)design process, your goal should be to generate as many alternatives as you can. Ten, twenty or more would be a good target. The most important thing to remember is that no assumption is sacred. Again, the online Canvanizers can be incredibly helpful, because you can move any element of the business model into any other area or even out of the model entirely and into the 'brainstorm' area at the bottom. You can generate an almost endless set of new business model elements in that brainstorm area and then try them in various parts of the model.

If you are looking for some brainstorm guidance, check out the IDEO Brainstorming Excursion.

Finally, you will want intuition-based ideas as well. It is probably impossible to completely clear your mind of the assumptions you have about the opportunity. Do the best you can to rely on intuition as well as generate ideas outside your comfort area. Working off the information you get from experts and non-experts may give you excellent, unexpected business model elements.

Quantity matters much more than quality at this stage. We encourage students and entrepreneurs to record every idea, no matter how silly some of them might seem at first glance. Some of the most interesting ideas result from building on or adjusting ideas that seem non-viable at the start. You can build only on what you record. After all, it is easy to cross out, delete or otherwise ignore ideas later.

Test

Ultimately, a business model is only as good as its implementation.

In the BMC process, we aspire to test as much of the proposed business model as possible to inform and guide implementation. The most time-intensive step is generally testing the model. There are three types of tests in the BMC: thought experiments, informational tests and pilot tests.

Think carefully about your (re)design. Some new business models can be tested only in practice, which requires piloting specific organisational activities to generate feedback from customers, partners or even competitors. If you are headed down that path, can you adjust the (re) design to facilitate thought or informational experiments first?

Thought experiments

A thought experiment is a mental walkthrough of the change process and the expected results. Entrepreneurs and managers engage in thought experiments all the time, most commonly by exploring the question: 'What if?'

The BMC benefits from both open-ended exploration as well as process-driven analysis. The 'What if?' experiments based on (re)design will be most effective when we have considered a variety of possible changes and then apply a clear set of metrics and goals to evaluate the tests.

There is, unfortunately, no complete set of questions to facilitate all possible business model thought experiments. Table 13.3 provides a series of questions, based on the RTVN framework, that give you a useful starting point for generating your own thought experiments.

TABLE 13.3 Thought experiments

Resources	▪ What if we had to use a different key resource? ▪ What if we had to find alternative key activities to generate value or reach customers? ▪ What if we could work with any partner company/entity in the world? Who would we choose? Why? ▪ What if we could generate a perfect resource (asset, person, capital) to create more value? What would it look like? ▪ What if we could leverage our operations/activities to generate a new, unique, valuable resource, separate from what we provide to customers?
Transactions	▪ What if we had to find a different channel to reach customers? ▪ What if our cost of customer interaction were zero? What if our cost of customer interaction were 10 × what it is now? ▪ What if we could target any customer segment, without considering the size of the segment, adoption tendencies or profitability? ▪ What if we could change the market itself? How would we change it? ▪ What if we could change one thing about all of our customers? What would we change?

Values	▪ What if we had to cut 25 per cent out of our cost structure? What about 50 per cent? ▪ What if we could raise our prices by 2 ×? What if we had to lower our prices by 50 per cent? ▪ What single element of value do our customers want that we do not currently provide? ▪ What value will our customers want in five years, even if they do not know it now?

If you are looking for more creative inspiration, you might check out the Oblique Strategies Excursion at the book website.

The Thought Experiment Excursion at the book website can also provide guidance on how to ensure that your thought experiments generate useful results.

Information tests

Information tests should, generally, be precise data queries that address a specific thought experiment.

For example: a key question for Adam Sutcliffe in commercialising the Orbel hand sanitiser was whether the device could be manufactured for roughly the same price as standard dispensers. Another key question was whether the health services (hospitals and clinics) market was more attractive than the consumer market. As you can see, these questions have very different scope and investment requirements. Answering the first might be straightforward to someone with product engineering and manufacturing experience, but finding the right person might take time. The second question requires much more information about customers, markets and market entry costs. It would be better to narrow the question significantly and confirm whether this is an important thought experiment. At the time, we referred to this as the 'American Soccer Mom' question. Would American mothers pay more for a hand sanitiser that was easy to transport and could be used one-handed?

Information tests are valuable when:

1. They can be answered quickly with limited resources.
2. The results are likely to be meaningful for the (re)design process.

In some cases, the critical path for exploiting an opportunity may invalidate some information tests. Consider Orbel again. When advising Sutcliffe on commercialisation paths, one of the key challenges was identifying a professional managers to lead the process. Sutcliffe never wanted to be CEO. He was not looking forward to the administrative and operational responsibilities of product launch. At one point, we discussed a team that included successful executives from the medical device and health services industries. It was clear, in talking with this team, that their initial target would be the health services industry rather than consumers. This made sense given their experience and networks.

One possibility, in this type of situation, is to do the market and customer research before selecting the team. Sutcliffe did not have the resources (time and money) to do the kind of customer and market analysis required. Ultimately, the biggest driver of the Orbel commercialisation effort was the selection of the commercialisation team.

Pilot tests

The most powerful (re)design tests are pilot tests. Here, the entrepreneur or organisation finds a way to test hypotheses, information, products or even entire business models in the real world.

A great example of real-time hypothesis testing took place at FanDuel. FanDuel, originally based in Edinburgh, is now one of the two largest online fantasy sports betting sites. Formed by the development team and investors from a failed social networking venture, FanDuel chose an opportunity (fantasy sports betting) and figured out the business model as it went. Tom Griffiths, co-founder and chief product officer, described the first couple of years as putting every kind of daily game they could think of onto the website to see what customers actually were willing to join. During the first years, FanDuel lived in constant pilot test mode. Did customers prefer to build a team for a day or did they want to keep rosters for a week? Did they want to bet directly against other sports fans? For example, did a Manchester United fan specifically want to bet against a City fan? How important were team loyalties to the participants? What kind of information did customers want and use to make decisions? What kind of information led customers to participate in more leagues? Tom described being deluged in data, trying to figure out what worked, without overloading the team or the web servers. FanDuel was a venture that had the timing exactly right – it rode the wave of a massive, exploding market.

You can read about a simpler, smaller example in the Ocere Excursion at the book website.

A pilot test puts as much as possible of your product or service in front of customers. Pilot testing works well in some, but not all industries. It can be extremely effective in online contexts, where the cost of changing content and process is relatively low. It is nearly impossible in heavily regulated industries, such as medical devices.

Entrepreneurs sometimes balk at pilot testing. Why? To some entrepreneurs, it feels like it is the final step into reality. This is, however, the single most counter-productive mindset for an entrepreneur to have.

The pilot test is often the final opportunity to recognise a dead end before it is too late. Missing a chance to pilot test your product or service is the equivalent of buying a car without test-driving it. No matter how good it looks on paper, you will not know for certain until the rubber hits the road.

'Make what you can sell, don't just try to sell what you have made.'

Jose Estabil, former president of tau-Metrix and senior director of technology at KLA-Tencor (personal interview)

Great pilot tests all have two characteristics in common. First, pilot tests should be simple to implement and simple to unwind. Sometimes that will mean telling alpha customers that the product, service or business model is still in beta-testing and could be withdrawn. Some entrepreneurs have expressed the concern that they could burn bridges with potential customers by showing them a half-baked idea. This is an appropriate but misdirected concern. If the relationship with the potential customer is so fragile that one misstep will wreck it, then that customer should not be included in the pilot test. Further, the venture should be seeking to build stronger relationships with customers in which the customer buys into the entire business model, not just a product feature.

Simplicity means that only the most limited resources will be leveraged to put the product or service in front of potential customers. It means that if the customer begins to ask complex questions or require complex assistance, the test has already been partly completed. Note that this does not mean that the test has 'failed'. There is no *failure* in a pilot test – only different types of informational outcomes.

Finally, simplicity means that if the information gathered in the pilot test begins to point towards significant or complex changes in the business model, the test is again complete. Pilot tests should be focused on either identifying incremental modifications to make a business model viable or establishing that the model needs significant revision.

Second, pilot tests should be focused. As any good scientist will attest, the trick to a great experiment is to limit the number of variables, especially variables you cannot control. If you want to find out how long it takes ice cubes to melt, you use a controlled environment with a constant temperature. You do not simply put the ice cubes outside on a variety of different weather days to see what happens. If you want to find out if your business model works, provide the simplest version you can to customers and limit the impact of external factors when they try it.

(Re)deploy

It may seem strange to wait to talk about (re)deploying the business model launch until Part 4 of this book. After all, most entrepreneurs *start* by launching a business model.

There is a lot to be said for getting in front of customers quickly and fixing problems as they emerge. In our entrepreneurship courses, we strongly encourage students to use the Lean Startup model wherever possible.

Presumably, however, you are reading this book precisely because you sought some insight and guidance on developing and implementing your business model. The 'build first, test later' philosophy can be powerful and effective, but it can also send entrepreneurs down time-consuming dead ends, especially if the 'build' effort does not have a clear end point.

Jose Estabil mentors entrepreneurs at MIT's Deshpande Center for Technological Innovation. In his professional career, he brought numerous critical technologies to market in the fast-moving and competitive semiconductor industry. His sage advice provides the key balancing element to the Lean Startup methodology. Get in front of customers and do your best to figure out what they want to buy and how they want to buy it. *Launching your business model does not mean you are tied to that business model forever.* But it does mean investing your reputation in a business model, at least for a while.

(Re)deploying a business model has similarities to launching a new product or service. Many of the entrepreneurs we mentor find the following analogy helpful.

Imagine that, for whatever reason, you want to sell your business. What is it that an acquirer is really buying? In certain highly specialised cases, an acquirer might want to buy only inventory, IP or even information such as a customer list. Ironically, what the acquirer probably needs *least* are the structures and formal components of your business, such as the legal entity and the relationships with service providers. What does the acquirer really want? Most likely, the acquirer is buying your business model. The acquirer wants the sum total of your operations, which should exceed the sum of the value of all the parts. It is the combination of resources, transactions and value creation that makes acquisitions attractive. It may take a bit of a stretch, but you can think of your business model itself as a *product.*

When you (re)deploy your business model, you are, in effect, relaunching that product (your organisation) into a new market. Yes, that 'product' includes the sale of specific products or services to your customers. But, at a higher level, your business model is a product in a large-scale market for organisations. If your new business model creates more value in that organisational market, then the (re)design and (re)deploy processes have succeeded.

There are, unfortunately, no guarantees when you (re) deploy a business model. In Chapter 14, we will look at the drivers of business model change and the key factors that support successful business model innovation. Effectively implementing a viable business model or business model innovation is mostly careful planning, clear execution and active monitoring.

> **Worksheet 13.1**
>
> **(RE)DEPLOY CHECKLIST**
>
> Download this worksheet for a detailed checklist for your (re)deploy effort based on the RTVN framework. You can use it even if you used one of the other canvas tools for your (re)design. Whilst it cannot guarantee success, it gives you a process to make sure you are on track.

One good option for (re)deploying your business model is simply to work with the new canvas you created in the (re) design stage. For each element of the canvas, you should be able to answer the following questions:

- How is this element different from the current operational state?
- What investments must be made, resources acquired or processes changed to implement the new element?
- What are the critical steps to initiate this change? Has responsibility for each step been assigned to a specific person or group?

- What impediments or hindrances must be overcome?
- What measure will demonstrate that the change has been accomplished?

The business model cycle provides an important overlay to generating business models. Throughout this book, we have seen that business models provide a flexible approach to understanding and improving organisational viability. Business model analysis encourages non-traditional thinking; any organisational element could be changed or eliminated. The BMC framework helps put business model design into a broader context. Effective business models are dynamic constructs that need to be constantly tested against market and industry conditions. In the next chapter, we will investigate how and why organisations change business models, what distinguishes business model change from business model innovation and the conditions that drive successful business model innovation.

RECAP

- Business models are dynamic; there needs to be a process to continually revisit them.
- The business model cycle has four steps: troubleshoot, (re)design, test and (re)deploy.
- Effective business models require open-ended exploration as well as a process-driven analysis that tests against the RTVN framework.

14 Business model change and innovation

'Business model innovations have reshaped entire industries and redistributed billions of dollars of value.'

Johnson, Christensen, and Kagermann

'Business model innovation is risky . . . [it] is a leap of faith based on limited, unknowable information . . . like jumping off a mountain.'

Bock and George

Business models fail.

Sometimes, it is neither the product, the service, the team nor the execution. Sometimes, *it really is the business model.*

Remember independent travel agents? Music stores that sold (new) LPs, cassettes and CDs? Video rental stores like Blockbuster? Bits and pieces of these industries still exist (Thomas Cook, local 'vinyl' shops, Family Video in the USA), but the business models that supported large numbers of firms or facilities in these industries simply do not work any more. Remember small, local internet services providers (ISPs) offering modem-based dial-up?

Business models change for the same reason that everything else about business changes. Schumpeter's vision of 'creative destruction' is more evident and vibrant now than it has ever been. New ideas, technologies and processes generate a continuous churn of resources, transactions and values. As some products and services become more popular, others must be abandoned.

For further thoughts on this, please see the Creative Destruction Excursion at the book website.

In this chapter, we will clarify the concepts of business model change and business model innovation. We will discuss the risks and rewards of initiating these processes. Finally, we will explore the reasons that business models change and the likely drivers for successful business model innovation.

The difference between business model change and business model innovation

Business model change appears straightforward. If the business model is different, then business model change has taken place.

'If you're going to put your product in beta – put your business model in beta with it.'

Joe Kraus, Google Ventures

Yet neither scholars nor managers rely on this simple perspective. There is an implicit understanding in much of the literature and practice of business models that small, incremental or isolated changes in any one element of a business model do not, technically, represent business model change.

Consider the example of a business that provides back-end data management services to manufacturing and retail customers. Some processes and jobs are repetitive and consistent but cannot be completely standardised. The executive team decides to begin outsourcing the repetitive work rather than retaining in-house resources. Is this a business model change? Based on the simplest definition, we would have to say yes. The reality, however, is that most entrepreneurs and managers consider this to be a simple resource or supplier change. Outsourcing a non-core or non-critical activity, just as an example, does not seem to warrant the stamp of 'business model change'.

For consistency with both the literature and our observations of practice, we will adopt this slightly more sophisticated approach to business model change. We define business model change as: 'the implementation of non-trivial changes to at least two business model elements.'

This helps clarify the difference between business model change and minor changes in operations, strategy, product, process or market. A great business model is more than the sum of its parts. If changing one element of a business model has no appreciable effect on the rest of the model, then it seems reasonable to argue that the overall business model has not really changed.

What about business model innovation (BMI)? Clearly, business model innovation is a specialised case of business model change. BMI needs to meet the criteria for business model change and also some criteria for novelty. In our academic research, we defined BMI as 'the development of novel configurations of resources and transactions to create new markets or serve markets in new ways.' We think this is still accurate. For simplicity and consistency we will use an adjusted definition in this book.

The challenge here is defining 'innovation'. Is a business model innovative if the company has never tried it before? Is it innovative only if it has not been used in the local industry? Or is it innovative only if no one on the planet has ever tried it before? Clearly, we could get caught in a semantics argument!

When it comes to business models, context is important. If an organisation is testing out a business model that it has seen a competitor use, it is not really innovative. If, on the other hand, the entrepreneur is trying a business model that has never been used in that industry or with its current customers, then it would seem to be an innovation.

Business model innovation is *the implementation of non-trivial changes to at least two business model elements resulting in a business model configuration that is new to the organisation's industry and market.*

What if the entrepreneur has seen that business model used in another industry? We believe it is still innovative because some or many business model elements will not transfer from one industry to another. In other words, the entrepreneur will still be implementing a new business model.

Note, however, that there is no completely objective measurement or judgement for 'business model innovation'. The next time you read about an example of 'business model innovation' in popular media, you might consider whether it meets the criteria we have proposed. It is unlikely there will ever be perfect consensus on business model innovation; after all, there is no perfect consensus on business models!

The risks and rewards of business model innovation

Who cares? Maybe business model innovation is not really a big deal.

Preliminary studies, and our own observations, suggest that it *is* a big deal.

Business model innovation is a high-risk, high-return proposition.

Business model *change* may be relatively incremental, focused on adapting the organisation to a changing industry or market context. Or it might emphasise incremental process improvement to increase operational efficiencies. Business model *innovation*, however, requires the organisation to act entrepreneurially, with a willingness to change any business model element no longer fit for purpose.

'Unlike product and process innovation, business model innovation must be both opportunity-centric ***and*** *disruptive. BMI requires a fundamental change in how the firm generates and captures value.'*

Bock and George

Business model innovation can be a powerful mechanism for creating advantage. The most well-known example is, of course, Apple, which used business model innovation to go from bankruptcy in 1997 to the most valuable company in the world only 15 years later in 2012. In the process, Apple transformed the music, telephone and computer industries.

The value of business model innovation was recognised as early as 2007. The results of IBM's Global CEO survey demonstrated that outperforming companies were relying on business model innovation over product and process innovation. Check out the Global CEO Survey Excursion for more results from that large-scale, global study.

Business model innovation has truly come into its own. Some estimates suggest that the majority of large companies have explored some business model innovation. The companies that have generated the highest growth and value creation used business model innovation.

'Fully 11 of the 27 companies born in the last quarter century that grew their way into the Fortune 500 in the past 10 years did so through business model innovation.'

Johnson, Christensen and Kagerman

At the same time, business model innovation comes with a steep price. Thousands of companies have gambled unsuccessfully on business model innovation. Most are completely lost to study. A few, such as Napster, are iconic for the catastrophic nature of their failure. For another great example, read the GeoCities Excursion at the book website.

To date, there are no rigorous studies of either the cost of business model innovation or business model innovation failure rates. Anecdotally, however, we have seen far more failures than successes, especially for growth-stage technology companies. These organisations, like Voxel in online content hosting and Savage Entertainment in video game development, tried to implement novel business models in highly competitive spaces. Both companies ultimately were acquired (rather than failed), but the acquisitions were driven by unsuccessful business model innovation and the near-term prospect of organisational failure.

The problem with business model innovation is simple. It requires the organisation to invest in an (at least partly) untested opportunity. In most cases, there is no going back because those investments will take the company away from the value creation processes it has relied on. Consider Barnes & Noble's push into the e-reader industry. The Barnes & Noble NOOK struggled against Amazon's Kindle, but was heavily supported through launch in both the USA and the UK. Although there is no publicly available information on the total investment to launch and support NOOK, Microsoft's initial commitment of $600m and Pearson's investment of $90m provide a sense of scale. In 2016, Barnes & Noble (B&N) announced the closing of the NOOK App store, acknowledging that the western world had standardised to the Google, Apple and Amazon app platforms. Many analysts suggested that the NOOK did not have the platform support or the novelty to compete with Amazon and Google. In the meantime, whilst B&N remains the largest bookstore chain in the USA, it continues to suffer losses and close stores. Estimates for B&N's total losses attributable to the NOOK range from a few hundred million dollars to well over a billion dollars.

'[Business model innovation] success derives in part from truly novel approaches to value creation and implementation of drastic changes in organizational processes, resources, and systems. These commitments are a gamble that may lock the firm into hard-to-change projects, assets, and capabilities.'

Bock and George

In the remainder of this chapter, we will explore the drivers of business model innovation and the factors that lead to successful business model innovation. Using IBM's Global CEO dataset, we discovered some remarkable findings about business model innovation. For more information about our research, read the Agile Business Model Innovation Excursion at the book website.

Drivers of business model innovation

Why do companies engage in business model change and innovation in the first place? The hard truth is that change is inevitable; companies that cannot adapt risk obsolescence.

'There's not a single business model . . . There are really a lot of opportunities and a lot of options and we just have to discover all of them.'

Tim O'Reilly, the 'Oracle of Silicon Valley' and founder of O'Reilly Media

As we noted in Chapter 12, a key driver of business model change is often the recognition of underperformance that cannot be attributed to a single operational factor. Business model innovation may also be driven by opportunity recognition. Anecdotally, almost anything can spur efforts to adapt and innovate a business model. The IBM data, however, showed that specific factors spur business model innovation efforts.

We will briefly review those factors here. More detailed information can be found in the Drivers of BMI Excursion as well as in our book *Models of Opportunity*.

Table 14.1 summarises which factors drive business model innovation:

- BMI is independent of sector and industry as well as organisation size. No specific industry or operational scale generates more business model innovation.
- Homogeneous or focused organisations are more likely to try business model innovation. Global organisations and organisations that span cultures (e.g. firms in the EU) are less likely.

TABLE 14.1 Drivers of business model innovation

	Driver of business model innovation?	
	Yes	No
Sector/Industry		X
Organisation size		X
Narrow or focused organisational culture/goals	X	
Local market trends		X
Global trends/distant exploration	X	
Executive leadership	X	
Product/process innovators		X
Prior change success		X

- The only external factor consistently linked to business model innovation is globalisation. Firms directly addressing globalisation challenges are more likely to try business model innovation.
- Senior leadership, especially CEO leadership, encourages more business model innovation.
- Companies heavily engaged in product or process innovation are less likely to be business model innovators.
- Prior successful change is not linked to business model innovation.

The key drivers of business model innovation are challenges that engage the organisation's long-term, core value propositions. On the one hand, this matches our expectations that small, specific changes in operations and strategy should not be called 'business model change'. On the other, it reinforces that business model innovation is not for the faint of heart. The companies that initiate serious business model innovation efforts accept that the viability of the organisation is at stake, tied to the need for fundamental change.

When business model innovation succeeds

No one has done more to explore and explain business model innovation than Professor Henry Chesbrough. He has generated extensive and thoughtful research that addresses the promise and peril of business model innovation.

'[B]usiness model innovation is vitally important, and yet very difficult to achieve.'

Henry Chesbrough

We know that successful business model innovation leads to outperformance. Getting to successful business model innovation, however, requires that organisations stay agile. BMI is a leap in the dark because firms must tackle unfamiliar challenges. To make BMI work, firms need the agility to adjust to changing conditions and new information.

Our research revealed a two-stage process for remaining agile during business model innovation. Remember that business model innovation is not easy. If it were, every firm would do it successfully. If you are going to implement BMI, keep an open mind. Individuals, groups and departments will need flexibility, good humour and the support of management to participate effectively in business model change processes. Remember that recognising business model innovation opportunities is not obvious. The best ideas may come from unexpected places!

'Fact is, inventing an innovative business model is often mostly a matter of serendipity.'

Gary Hamel

The two-stage business model innovation plan

'Business model innovators do far more than adjust strategic positioning; they exploit non-intuitive entrepreneurial opportunities that become obvious only in hindsight. BMI is a leap of faith based on limited, unknowable information.'

Bock and George

If you have come this far and concluded that your organisation needs to consider business model innovation, you have a daunting task in front of you. You should size up the opportunity and the capabilities of your organisation but, at some point, you will have to take the leap of faith. If you succeed, hindsight will make your success appear obvious to others; if you fail, it may be difficult or impossible to recover.

Figure 14.1 shows the two-stage BMI Tool. In stage 1, the firm uses CEO leadership, distant exploration and a plan for discontinuous change to get the BMI process started. Once the organisation has committed to business model innovation, the stage 2 factors help implement BMI successfully.

> **Worksheet 14.1**
>
> **THE TWO-STAGE BMI TOOL**
>
> Download this worksheet for a process and readiness checklist. The questions to ask are on the worksheet and discussed through the rest of this chapter.

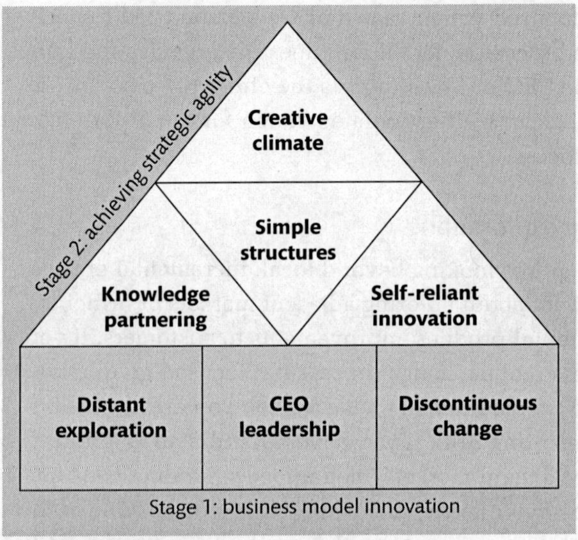

FIGURE 14.1 The two-stage BMI tool

Stage 1: leveraging the key drivers of business model innovation

In stage 1, your goal should be to ensure that your organisation is prepared to initiate business model innovation. You will need motivation and commitment from the top management team, the vision to look at entirely new, long-term opportunities and the drive to consider radical change at the organisation.

CEO leadership

You, or whoever leads the organisation, must assume a prominent, enthusiastic and optimistic position to cheerlead the BMI process. It is not essential for the CEO (MD or other top leader) to supervise the entire BMI process from start to finish. However, the key thought leader must ensure that the entire organisation is committed to one clear, focused vision. Has that key person been the driver for the process so far? If not, does the organisation know that the CEO or MD supports the effort 100 per cent? Is there a clear, well-articulated vision for the BMI outcome and process?

Distant exploration

BMI requires looking beyond local, incremental change. BMI is not about entering adjacent markets or bringing incremental product improvements to customers. If your business model change process has focused on relatively simple or incremental changes, then you are not really implementing BMI. If you have not initiated an effort to explore distant markets, technologies, product concepts and customer needs, this is the time to do so. One of the worst things your organisation could do is implement BMI halfway. When the job is done, you may discover that one of your competitors or a new entrant has gone the full distance and leapfrogged your results. Have you taken the time to consider where customers, markets and industries will be in 5 years? 10 years? 20 years? What efforts have been made to consider opportunities well outside the organisation's current value proposition? What new companies do you imagine competing with in 5 years? 10 years? 20 years? If they are the same companies you compete with now, are you really considering BMI?

Discontinuous change

Most organisational capabilities benefit from experience. BMI may not. Prior successful change is not linked to successful BMI. It may be that BMI cannot be learned over time. Each BMI initiative is unique.

Is your organisation prepared for discontinuous change? Have you prepared key people for new and unfamiliar responsibilities? Will your physical and information facilities be able to accommodate new activities and monitoring processes? Once the most aggressive and disruptive changes have been identified, who will be responsible for supporting the employees most affected?

Stage 2: preparing the organisation for successful business model innovation

If the stage has been set, there are four factors linked to successful business model innovation. You will need to maintain a creative climate, strive to simplify organisational structures, partner for knowledge about opportunities and ensure self-reliance for innovations.

Creative climate

The most critical factor in successful business model innovation is creative culture at the organisation. Business model innovation requires the organisation to take on new challenges, implement new activities and potentially address completely new ways of creating value. A creative, innovation-friendly culture provides the foundation for addressing change.

Without a creative, flexible organisational climate, BMI will be difficult to implement. How does climate at your organisation compare to other firms in the industry? Have you conducted a climate survey recently? If the climate is not conducive to significant change, do you have the ability to delay BMI, even temporarily, to better prepare your organisation? Regardless of the climate level, what steps could you take to encourage flexible and creative thinking and behaviour?

Simple structures

Business model innovation usually requires significant change to both high-level and operational activities. The change process will be more efficient and effective when the organisation can focus on core functions and responsibilities.There are, however, subtle challenges in the need for simplicity. Simply eliminating non-core functions (via sale or spin-off) can actually hinder business model innovation. The challenge is focusing management attention on key functions and activities without losing access to external information about changing markets and opportunities. Careful partnering can be a key part of this process.

If you are going to implement BMI, carefully consider how to be a delegator. Create a prioritised list of groups, large-scale activities, or key processes that your business currently relies on. The best list would include between 5–10 groups and processes. Once it is prioritised, carefully consider whether some or many of the less critical elements could be delegated to other, trusted organisations. The delegation process frees up managerial capabilities within your organisation. You do not want to give up control of those processes; you especially want to ensure that you have access to market information through your partners. Are you really freeing up managerial attention or are you just reconfiguring internal activities? One of the surprising things we learned in our research was that delegating helped BMI, but simply reconfiguring resources actually hindered BMI.

To see a fascinating example of restructuring, the 'Fractal' business model Excursion at the book website.

Partnering for knowledge

Business model innovation will likely require moving your organisation into new sectors, customer segments or even entirely new markets. Beyond delegating non-core functions, what opportunities do you have to partner for knowledge in those new fields? Think about the potential customers you most want to serve if your BMI is successful. What combination of capabilities and resources would increase the probability that they would get value from your BMI outcomes? What firms could help provide those capabilities and resources? Can you reach out to those organisations to facilitate your entry into new sectors and markets?

Self-reliance for innovation

Ultimately, successful BMI results from internally generated ideas. It helps to partner with people and firms to ensure that you have the most up-to-date information on opportunities. In the end, however, only your firm can be responsible for the innovations and changes that fuel effective BMI. What internal incentives do you have to generate those innovations? What incentives do you have to help people embrace the changes necessary to make BMI work? How will everyone at your organisation benefit from self-reliant innovation? Do they all know that?

In our book about BMI, *Models of Opportunity,* we discuss Return Path, the world's leading email marketing whitelist company. Return Path partnered with global ISPs to obtain data on the characteristics of emails that go to users' inboxes and emails that are redirected to junk or spam folders. This information has been critical, but Return Path did not rely on the ISPs to generate its novel business model for email marketing services and its email whitelist database. Those innovations came from constant efforts to explore distant possibilities in the email industry combined with an incredibly creative and supportive climate for innovation within the organisation. As just one example, the company allowed all employees to give small, instant rewards ($25) to other employees for exceptional work. These were provided through an automated process that did not require approval from senior managers. Many of the company's novel product and service improvements had their origins in a $25 idea.

Learn more about these key factors in the Drivers of Successful BMI Excursion.

Business model innovation is one part terror and one part exhilaration. If you are living on the edge of your seat, the odds are you are doing it right. From all of us who have been through BMI at one time or another, successfully or not – good luck and Godspeed!

RECAP

- Business model innovation is a high-risk, high-reward effort.
- BMI is not driven by industry, organisation size, local market trends or prior change success.
- Firms focused on product or process innovation are less likely to initiate business model innovation.
- Firms that initiate BMI tend to have active CEO leadership, a willingness to look at distant opportunities and a narrow focus or homogeneous culture.
- Successful BMI requires a creative culture, simple structures, partnering for knowledge and self-reliance for innovation.
- When it comes to business model innovation, there are no guarantees.

15 Sustainable business models

*'[A sustainable business model] must be **part of a sustainable society.** It is not possible to be a sustainable business in an unsustainable economy. All business models rely on particular external conditions; to be called sustainable, those conditions must match with a thriving economy that is delivering social progress within environmental limits.'*

David Bent, Forum for the Future

What does 'sustainable' or 'sustainability' mean in the context of business models?

In this chapter, we will explore the concept of a 'sustainable business model'. We will show how you can choose to incorporate or ignore sustainability elements in your own ventures. Building sustainability into your business model is a *choice* driven by the personal beliefs and values of entrepreneurs and managers.

There is not sufficient space in this book to address ethics, globalisation, justice or human rights. Please read the Sustainability Excursion for additional thoughts on this, including how we reference 'ecology' and 'social good'.

Unpacking the 'sustainable business model'

So, what is a *sustainable business* model? We will use that phrase because it has become convenient and convention to do so. What does a sustainable business model mean to you?

> **Worksheet 15.1**
>
> **UNPACKING SUSTAINABLE BUSINESS MODELS**
>
> To get the most out of this chapter, please download Worksheet 15.1 from the BMB website. Follow along as we unpack this tricky phrase. To start, write down your own definition for a 'sustainable business model' in box #1. Do not skip ahead to page 2 of the worksheet!

The sustainable 'business model'

Probably the simplest interpretation is the idea of a sustainable (pause) 'business model'. That is: a business model that is sustainable. What does 'sustainable' mean here?

Go to box #2 on the worksheet. Think about this idea of a business model that is sustainable. What does that mean to you? Is it at all different from what you wrote in box #1?

The simplest definition for a sustainable 'business model' is one that will last over time.

In effect, we are talking about competitive advantage. The sustainable business model has been used by scholars to emphasise how a firm maintains a long-term edge over competitors.

'The opportunity has an attractive, sustainable business model; it is possible to create competitive edge and defend it.'

Sahlman 1997

'Strategy analysis is thus an essential step in designing a competitively sustainable business model.'

Teece 2010

Did you write about strategy or time-based competition in box #2? Regardless, do you see why these scholars have interpreted it this way?

The 'sustainable business' model

Next is a slightly different perspective: the 'sustainable business' (pause) model. Here we seem to be emphasising something different – a model of a sustainable business. What does that mean?

Go to box #3 on the worksheet. Think about this idea of a model of a sustainable business. What does that mean to you? Write down your definition in box #3.

It appears that we are now talking about some sort of map, representation or instruction set for a sustainable business. And we never even agreed on what a 'sustainable business' was!

'A sustainable business model is a roadmap for achieving sustainability and deals with the issues and dynamic relationships of sustainability dimensions of the businesses.'

Ahmed and Sundaram 2007

Did you write something in box #3 about business or organisational elements that deal with sustainability? Did you clarify what sustainability means in that context? We could still be talking about viability or longevity, but it seems as if we are talking about something slightly different – something to do with ecological impact or social benefit.

Some scholars and consultants have tried to clarify this distinction by talking about 'sustainability business' rather than 'sustainable business'. Please read the Sustainability Business Excursion to explore this distinction.

As you can see, the phrase 'sustainable business model' is really shorthand for something much more complicated. Let us try to figure it out.

The 'sustainable business' 'business model'

Now we are talking about a 'sustainable business' (pause) 'business model'. This appears to be a business model for something we are calling a sustainable business.

Go to the worksheet and write down in box #4 what this phrase means to you.

'[F]irm-level sustainability and. . . sustainability for the system that an organization is part of.'

Stubbs and Cocklin 2008

We seem to have addressed most of the issues here. This incorporates an ecological aspect to the organisation's business model. And we can even sneak in the idea that sustainability also has something to do with the broader industrial community, social context or biosphere in which the business model functions. But now we have lost that element of longer-term viability.

The sustainable 'sustainable business' 'business model'

Is this where we meant to be all along? This (awful) phrase should be read as: the sustainable (pause) 'sustainable business' (pause) 'business model'. This describes a business model, for a sustainable business, where the business model is sustainable. Go to box #5 on the worksheet and write down what this means to you.

How did we get here? We wanted the 'sustainability' element to refer to both the nature of the business itself and also to the idea that the business model should be viable over the long haul.

Perhaps you are wondering if this last element of viability is really necessary. We think it is: we could generate business models that incorporate sustainability but are clearly noncompetitive. There have been many of those firms – often led by a visionary entrepreneur with a specific ecological or social cause. These organisations briefly thrive and then collapse because the unique resource that allows the venture to function is the unpaid labour of the entrepreneur! There is not much sustainable about *that* business model.

How does this compare to what you had in mind at the start?

Would the real 'sustainable business model' please stand up?

'A sustainable business model is one in which the profit motive and environmental benefits are aligned. [A] sustainable business model . . . encourages "responsible consumerism", employee engagement, long-term relationships between customers, business and suppliers and a focus on the needs of customers. All of these should help to provide sustainable economic growth.'

Scottish Enterprise

What should we do with all these variations and explanations?

When we talk sustainable business models, we mean business models that are intrinsically linked to ecological issues, but also have long-term competitive viability.

A sustainable business model aligns the long-term viability of the organisation with the ecological system in which the organisation operates. Remember that a business model is the organisational design used to exploit an opportunity. In other words, we are still talking about how we design a venture, but now we are using a much wider lens for thinking about its impact.

A sustainable business model is an organisational design, used to exploit an opportunity, that aligns the viability of the organisation with the ecological and/or social system in which it operates. One example of this approach can be seen in TOMS shoes, which became famous for its buy-one give-one programme.

'The future of TOMS is really creating a whole new business model of this one-for-one giving and expanding the TOMS model from shoes into other products as well.'

Blake Mycoskie

For more about TOMS shoes, including a link to a video about why Blake Mycoskie started the company, take a look at the TOMS Excursion on the book website.

Ultimately, real sustainable business models will have to change over time because our understanding of what is sustainable is changing.

A great tool for thinking about sustainability, specifically in the context of business model innovation, is the business model innovation grid (Figure 15.1), produced by researchers at the Centre for Industrial Sustainability at Cambridge and supported by Plan C, the Flanders-based network promoting sustainable use of materials. The grid suggests sustainability innovations across three broad impact areas: technological, social and organisational. For example, a technological improvement in optimisation could involve de-materialising a product or its packaging. A social improvement focused on functionality rather than ownership could enable customers to pay for product use and then return it to the manufacturer for recycling rather than dispose of it themselves (probably to landfill). An organisational improvement emphasising social entrepreneurship could explore localisation of production and other activities rather than operational centralisation.

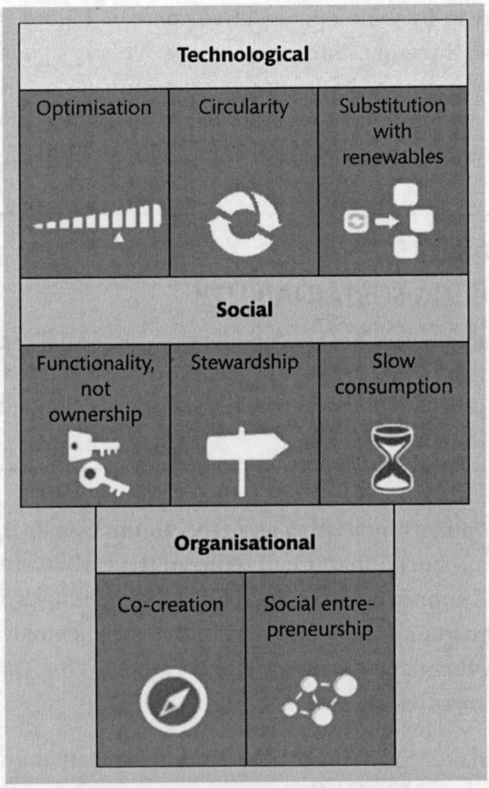

FIGURE 15.1 Business model innovation grid developed by Centre for Industrial Sustainability at Cambridge and Plan C

Source: Circular Flanders

Measuring sustainable business models

One of the core disagreements about sustainable business models is the right metric for determining sustainability.

The challenge is that we can examine sustainability from at least three perspectives: intent, process and outcome. This is not an issue of agreeing on ecological impact, carbon footprint, global climate disruption or whether (a certain level of) economic growth is ultimately good. Your assessment of whether a business model is sustainable may well be driven by which perspective you use. Figure 15.2 shows these three possible perspectives. This is a good opportunity to think about how you measure sustainability in your business model and whether or not you have previously had 'sustainability' as a goal for your business model.

Worksheet 15.2

MEASURING SUSTAINABILITY

Download this worksheet to consider how sustainability could be measured in your business model. Fill in the first row as best you can; it is OK to enter 'Not applicable' or 'Nothing currently' in any of the cells.

Consider Walmart (operating as ASDA in the UK). In 2015, Walmart announced that it had reduced the carbon emissions of its global supply chain by 28.2 million metric tons since 2010. That certainly seems like an impressive ecological outcome. Other ecologically oriented outcomes for Walmart have been reported as well.

Does that make Walmart's business model sustainable? It certainly has aged well: Walmart has continued growth

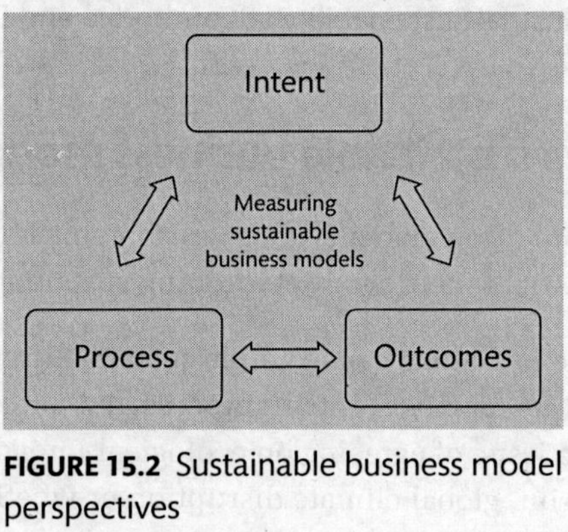

FIGURE 15.2 Sustainable business model perspectives

on a global level. But is it an ecologically sustainable business model? Whilst the final jury is arguably out, some observers have justifiably concluded that Walmart's total impact on global ecology is net negative: 'The sustainability measures Walmart has taken within its business model fail to compensate for the environmental harm inflicted by the business model as a whole.'

What about Walmart's intentions? The company has committed to a variety of positive ecological outcomes over the past 20 years, with varying levels of success. What about the process? One of the company's key steps to reducing carbon emissions was to encourage suppliers to find ways to reduce their carbon emissions, which represented 90 per cent of Walmart's total carbon footprint. Does it matter how those firms cut their emissions? If those activities resulted in other (unanticipated) negative ecological effects, would it diminish our evaluation of the sustainability of Walmart's business model?

The problem is that we can easily generate scenarios in which one perspective points towards a sustainable business model whilst another perspective suggests that the business model is not sustainable. What if a company intends to be sustainable but implements practices that unintentionally generate harm? What if an organisation has no sustainability intent at all but unintentionally generates overall ecological benefits?

Table 15.1 compares the three perspectives and addresses some of the theoretical and practical issues managers should consider.

Let us take another example: Olam International. Olam is a leading agri-business operating from seed to shelf in 70 countries, supplying food and industrial raw materials to over 23,000 customers worldwide. Its corporate headquarters is in Singapore, but it has over 70,000 employees across the world

TABLE 15.1 Sustainable business model perspectives

Perspective	Intent	Process	Outcomes
Frame of reference	Goals	Behaviour	Effects
What is 'measured'	Whether the organisation makes explicit qualitative and quantitative statements to be sustainable.	The choices and activities observed as the organisation addresses trade-offs.	Realised quantitative outcomes.
Sustainability theory	Long-term sustainability must be driven by organisational goal-making that connects the viability of the organisation with the ecological and/or social system.	Sustainability is achieved when organisations make real-world decisions that address trade-offs in the context of benefits to the ecological and/or social system.	Sustainability is achieved when organisations generate outcomes that are better for the ecological and/or social system than would otherwise have resulted.
Advantages	Easily observed and evaluated.	When implemented properly, incorporate specific rules for decision making that can be tested and copied.	Provides quantitative basis for assessment and comparison with other organisations and situations.
Disadvantages	Unclear threshold for sustainability intent; no requirement for action or outcomes; confusing means and ends; 'greenwashing'.	Difficult to generate rules, may require the organisation to work against its own self-interest or operate at a disadvantage to less 'sustainable' competitors; boundaries for measuring choices or activities; relative importance of activities and perceived impact.	Choice of metric may not be obvious; choice of timeframe may not be obvious; should outcomes be assessed in relative or absolute measures; small improvements may be used to hide larger problems or damages.

in many businesses including cocoa, coffee, cashew, rice and cotton. Olam's core business is in plantations and in trading; it ensures sustainable practices from the farm gate to the factory gate. Its innovations are around (reducing) water usage in farming practices, for example, by increasing solid content in onions by 5 per cent. This has several implications for reduced water usage for farming (by over 7 billion litres), dehydration and transport costs (by 8 million litres of diesel) and, more importantly, saves 800+ hectares of land. Sustainability is so integral to Olam's operations that it has championed the Global Agri-business Alliance to support the United Nations' Division of Sustainable Development (UN-DSD). This includes UN-DSD's goals to end poverty (goal 1), ensure access to water (goal 6), promote sustainable consumption and production (goal 12), combat climate change (goal 13), sustainably manage forests (goal 15) and revitalise partnerships for sustainable development (goal 17). These activities suggest that Olam has recognized that ecological sustainability is likely integral to the long-term sustainability of its business activities.

Entrepreneurs may develop business models that *intend* to be sustainable. Very often, entrepreneurs have an underlying motivation to accomplish a goal that is distinct from profit maximisation. For example, Matthew Golden wanted to reduce wasteful energy consumption on a large scale to help global ecology and decrease consumer energy costs.

In business model thinking, an intention is an organisational resource. It may be a vision statement, a goal or an effort to make the entrepreneur's tacit ideas explicit.

One challenge with the 'intent' perspective is identifying a minimum threshold. Most sustainability entrepreneurs have an implicit expectation for their goals. After all, if they only wanted incremental impact, they could simply change their own behaviour. Golden could have completed an energy audit on his own home and retrofitted it for energy savings.

But what is the right minimum threshold for a business model to be considered 'sustainable?'

Sustainable business model intent should distinguish between means and ends. Again, this is often implied but not explicit in many business models. Why? Sometimes the means and ends are difficult to clarify; sometimes the entrepreneur has not thoroughly examined her own intent. It is valuable to explore this because it will also drive the process aspect of a sustainable business model. When Adam Purvis created Power-Of-Youth (POY) to encourage successful entrepreneurs to pay their success forward, he was implicitly recognising that POY itself might not have a positive environmental or social impact. After all, it would use ecological resources without directly benefitting disadvantaged individuals. POY was purely a means-based sustainable business model; the intent is to propagate sustainability ideals to a much broader set of organisations.

Ultimately, the problem is that many organisations have learned to *say* good things about their own sustainability intentions. For publicly traded firms, often these can be found in statements of corporate social responsibility (CSR). Corporate statements about sustainability that do not seem to match behaviour or outcomes have been called 'greenwashing'.

Perhaps *process* is a better sustainable business model perspective. Process refers to what the organisation actually does. How does the organisation behave when there are trade-offs between sustainability outcomes and profit? It should be obvious that this ties closely to the activities and transactions within a business model framework.

Consider Golden's venture, Recurve. Developing the energy audit software required venture capital. Running the business required an office, which uses supplies. Recurve hoped to have significant long-term impact on home energy use in the USA and, eventually, around the world. Does that mean it should use sustainable practices throughout its business? The reality is that many sustainable practices (such as responsibly sourced office supplies) are more expensive than alternatives.

A key challenge is establishing boundaries. Where does the organisation draw the line for utilising and/or enforcing sustainable activities? Should the organisation require its partners and suppliers to adhere to similar rules or requirements? Recurve made significant efforts to utilise sustainable processes within its business model. It procured office supplies and equipment from organisations that had clear commitments to sustainable practices. It established employee support programmes to encourage low-carbon commuting activities.

How far do those boundaries extend? Should Recurve have monitored its partners and employees to expand the reach of its sustainability goals? What if some of its suppliers were not enforcing similar requirements on their partners and suppliers? This kind of monitoring and enforcement would have been expensive and time-consuming.

Should all activities be assessed equally? How deep does a business model need to go to align process with sustainable intent? Many organisational activities, such as office cleaning, appear relatively trivial. Does every activity at the organisation need to be analysed for sustainability?

The challenge of depth is tightly linked to the means/end aspect of intent. To see this more clearly, consider the case of US super-investor Warren Buffet. Buffet is considered one of the most successful business investors and managers in history. He has pledged to give away 99 per cent of his wealth to charitable causes. Although he has taken more liberal positions on issues of health care, taxes and wealth inequality, his company (Berkshire Hathaway) buys and operates businesses to generate and maximise profits. It is not immediately clear whether Buffet and his company take sustainability issues into account when considering investments. Is it better to (a) run a business without any sustainability depth at all and then donate the long-term profits to sustainability causes or (b) run a business with significant sustainable depth to create near-term sustainability benefits? There is no definitive answer to this question, but it is worth thinking about it for your own sustainable business model.

Two of our favourite examples where those priorities were made explicit are Recurve and Return Path. Both companies needed venture capital which is necessarily profit-focused. Yet both organisations had explicit priorities that inevitably would conflict with profit maximisation. Return Path had an employees-first mission and culture; Recurve was determined to use green processes, despite higher costs. Both companies eventually found venture capital firms that could buy into those visions. Those investors were willing to test the idea that such priorities could improve investment returns.

Finally, there is the *outcomes* perspective. This is where most sustainable business models start; an entrepreneur wants to improve ecology (or at least reduce ongoing damage) or have a positive impact on society. An outcomes perspective provides the most definitive tests for sustainable impact, but cannot address every issue.

For example, are sustainable outcomes absolute or relative? The Walmart example is almost certainly relative; the gains in energy efficiency and ecological impact are being measured against Walmart's impact *without* the sustainability initiatives. It would seem difficult to argue that Walmart's *absolute net impact* on global ecology is positive, taking into account total energy and resource use and waste production. Should Walmart get credit for improving? Or should it get credit only when its net effect is positive? How do we incorporate social impact? We can't fully assess this, but we note a few specific points on both sides. First, Walmart (via its subsidiary Sam's Club) has been identified as a top employer of individuals with disabilities. On the other hand, the company has faced discrimination lawsuits. Second, research has shown that Walmart stores adversely affect local retailers, local jobs and local growth. On the other hand, perhaps that means that capital is being more efficiently deployed and consumers are getting more of what they want at lower prices. It also might mean that profits are being channelled out of local areas into corporate hierarchies, which contributes to the growing rich-poor gap.

As you can see, evaluating business model sustainability outcomes presents a significant challenge, even if you are just trying to assess relative versus absolute impact.

One of the biggest problems is selecting outcome metrics. An ecological perspective might emphasise waste production or energy use. A social perspective might emphasise income or income equality, or measures such as access to education. Choosing metrics is closely linked to the priorities from the process perspective. You cannot measure everything, so every metric you select probably de-emphasises another metric.

Ultimately sustainable business models incorporate time

Our own instinct is that the real key to understanding sustainable business models has to do with timescale. Is your emphasis near-time impact or long-term effect? Is your timescale measured in months, years or decades?

Consider The SEED Foundation. SEED was created by Rajiv Vinnakota and Eric Adler in 1997 to address educational access in some of the USA's more disadvantaged cities. Its goal was to provide a high-quality education to middle-school students, starting at around age 11, who otherwise would be unlikely to finish high school. The timescale was not one year, or even five years. The 10-year goal was to help these students complete high school and college. But the Foundation had an even longer-term goal: to help revitalise these neighbourhoods by building a high-quality physical structure, providing local jobs and, ultimately, bringing college graduates back to the community.

When the timescale is long enough, it becomes possible to think about a business model's more holistic and extended impact.

This is a good time to dig deeper into your sustainable business model measures. If you have started Worksheet 15.2 already, reopen the file or find your printout. Try to fill out information about the measurement components. It is OK if you do not have a clear answer or feel you do not have enough information. Just thinking carefully through this process means you are further along than the vast majority of entrepreneurs and managers!

One of the best things you can do at this stage is to take your preliminary ideas about what makes your business model sustainable and share them with the smartest people you know. They might be industry experts, business colleagues or family members. Keep in mind that there are few, if any, definitive answers about large-scale sustainability. Talking with people you trust should generate questions and ideas that help you think about your business model or point towards new and innovative business models.

The study of sustainability and business models has only just started. We have studied over a dozen early stage technology companies across the world with sustainable aspects in their business models. Some of those companies have been very successful; some have failed. On the whole, we did not find that the sustainability elements were the critical factors in either success or failure. We suspect that clever entrepreneurs can find ways to make sustainable business models attractive, competitive and turn it into a performance advantage. At the same time, there is limited evidence that demonstrates ecological or social sustainability, on its own, is enough to guarantee success.

Our guidance for entrepreneurs and managers is simple. Look around you. Look at your own organisation, your community, your industry and your country. Does your work make any of them better, over time? When you hand them off to the next generation, will you be giving them more problems to solve or more opportunities to thrive? Will the next generation be happier and healthier because of your business model? Or will it have to work harder to achieve less, hindered by social and ecological damage?

Now, take a deep breath, step back and look at the planet. Note three things:

1. The Earth is the only thing you truly share with every other human being.
2. Unlike your organisation, your community, your industry and your country, you cannot leave the planet.
3. No matter what you do, the Earth is the only planet that will be available to the next generation. What will you leave behind?

Is your business model sustainable?

RECAP

- A 'sustainable business model' is shorthand to describe a business model that is intrinsically linked to ecological issues, but also has long-term competitive viability.
- Sustainability can be measured by intent, processes and/or outcomes.
- Thorough understanding of business model sustainability requires taking into account time and economic context.
- Right now, there are no universally accepted guidelines or parameters to definitely identify sustainable business models.

16 Back to business model basics

We have come a long way on our journey to design, build and adapt business models.

In this chapter, we will:

- Summarise and integrate that journey.
- Make a few notes about business models beyond for-profit businesses.
- Close the book with a few final tips.

Why business models matter

A great business model ties together resources, transactions and value creation. Developing great business models benefits from a variety of other management concepts and frameworks. The worksheets and activities in this book have guided you to create and assess numerous business models. You have all the tools to design, build and adapt business models for your own organisation.

'The most essential thing for us was to get the business model right, then put the world-class technology under it to support it. At Merrill, that meant not doing what people expected.'

John McKinley, former CTO at Merrill Lynch (personal correspondence)

The good news is that the business model is the single best indicator for whether your organisation is viable. Taking the time to generate and connect the elements of your current or new business model is a valuable and informative step towards business growth and success.

The bad news is that we cannot always predict why some business models work and others do not. Desk research can take your analysis only so far; some business models must be tested in the market. You have a variety of options for that testing process, ranging from thought experiments to implementing pilot tests. Those tests will be even more important if you are implementing business model innovation to generate entirely new business models.

A good idea is not enough

A great idea or innovation is not the same thing as a great business model. A business model addresses how the idea functions in a market context. There has to be some element of organisation to generate and distribute the idea and some transactive element to capture value. One of the most common mistakes made by entrepreneurs is believing that, if the idea is good enough, important enough, or just the 'right thing to do', somehow the business model will follow.

A good strategy can position the organisation effectively against competitors within the industry. Good people can ensure the organisation runs efficiently and leverages key resources. Creating value for users and customers can provide an opportunity for near- and long-term revenues. But unless they all fit together into a coherent business model, the organisation is probably not viable.

We started this book with Sal Khan's comment about not having a business model for Khan Academy. In fact, there *is* a business model there, focused on the idea that education should be universally accessible. We might all agree that from a perspective of social benefit or justice, universally accessible education is a good idea. But a good idea is not enough. The Khan Academy business model is incomplete: it has a strategy, great people and value creation. There is no question that Khan Academy serves a purpose and generates results. At the same time, there is no evidence yet that the Khan Academy business model can be sustained.

Sebastian Thrun noted that even a laudable enterprise like Khan Academy will ultimately need a business model that can be sustained over time. It is appealing to imagine that the global educational system could be remodelled around free content and free distribution. Today, however, Khan Academy is effectively a charity, dependent on year-to-year fundraising to cover costs.

Business models are not required to be 'nice'

Along with many other scholars and practitioners, we believe that entrepreneurship is one of the most important social phenomena of the modern age. We also believe that entrepreneurship has almost unbounded potential to improve the world, despite obvious cases of 'bad hats' and the dark side of entrepreneurial activity.

At the same time, there are no structural mechanisms to require businesses to consistently and holistically contribute to a better world. National and international legal frameworks provide only a limited system for restricting commercial organisations from causing harm. The burden is, for now, primarily individual and community-based.

Business models are not required to be nice.

Business models function within a larger economic context. Successful business models may create economic value whilst generating harm.

Consider the world of professional automobile racing (e.g. Formula 1, NASCAR). Racing interweaves a variety of organisations, users and customers in complex ways. Car companies participate for a variety of reasons, including research and development, brand bragging rights, competitive necessity and the potential for good PR and advertising value. Sponsors in the auto industry and beyond leverage the high profile events for advertising purposes. Drivers have a unique career experience, to say the least. What about customers? Why do people watch car racing? Whilst some enjoy the pure racing element and others are engaged with the industry and technology, some watch to see horrific crashes. The drama around possible cheating in some leagues may or may not contribute to the sport's appeal to viewers.

'. . . [Y]ou can kind of understand why those guys would really go outside the boundaries. It doesn't make it right and it doesn't mean that you're not going to get a big penalty if you get caught. It's risk versus reward, and I guess for those guys, they chose that that was enough . . . I hate it for the sport to see the focus get turned to that, but I will say the drama always outweighs just pure excitement. It seems to get more attention . . . The business model of racing is not a pretty one.'

Jeff Gordon.

Facebook, Google and other platforms have come under scrutiny and criticism for the various practices and policies around advertising. Do the organisations have a requirement to be responsible for the content shown to users, especially when those users are receiving services for free? At the moment, this is a question of ethics and social responsibility but has no direct or obvious *business* implications for their business models.

'A frustration I have is that a lot of people increasingly seem to equate an advertising business model with somehow being out of alignment with your customers. I think it's the most ridiculous concept.'

Mark Zuckerberg, CEO of Facebook

After all, if users perceived that they received net negative value as a result of the advertising practices, they would not use the service. And keep in mind that the *customers* of platforms like Facebook and Google are, in fact, those advertisers, not the consumers who *use* the platforms for social media or search. A user *uses*; a customer *pays*. The *customers* for the bulk of Google and Facebook services are advertisers! Some advertisers are beginning to wield that influence.

A similar story can be told about media networks, for example. Most media networks rely heavily on advertising for revenues, which offset the cost of producing or purchasing content (e.g. shows). As acclaimed producer Joss Whedon has pointed out, this is an example of a business model, including a purpose and structure. The content itself is partly irrelevant, because the model can function with many different types of content targeting many different viewer audiences. As Whedon notes, there isn't a moral or ethical judgement to be made here – the networks are simply using the model to make money, because ultimately the networks are business organisations.

To be sure, there are models for ad-free content and new entrants (e.g. Amazon, Apple) are testing out various business models. But, ultimately, there does have to be a business model, one that creates and captures value and can be sustained.

A similar tension can be seen in the news and printed content industries. Many newspapers have gone out of business as the internet changed how information is collected, evaluated and distributed. There is nothing 'fair' about business models, especially in industries undergoing dramatic change. We might decry the challenge faced by independent media outlets (e.g. *The Guardian*) or change in ownership (e.g. *The Independent*). We might be concerned about the success of business models that facilitate the creation and propagation of fake news; we might wonder how effective grass roots efforts can be to ensure that advertisers are aware of their support for questionable or fake content.

'Newspapers with declining circulations can complain all they want about their readers and even say they have no taste. But you will still go out of business over time. A newspaper is not a public trust – it has a business model that either works or it doesn't.'

Marc Andreessen

Ultimately, these are questions that go beyond how business models work or why they succeed. The questions of ethical and socially responsible behaviour cannot be addressed entirely within a business model framework. A business model functions within, and reflects, the reality of a larger context, including the dominant ethical and legal context. Successful business models are, ultimately, a reflection of what we, as a collective society, are willing to pay for.

Business models are about more than business

Although we have focused primarily on for-profit businesses in this book, business models are relevant for any organisation. If there is organisation, formal or informal, legal or illegal, for good or evil, for-profit or not-for-profit, there is a business model. And the same tools and frameworks apply; usually the key distinction is the definition of 'value'.

In fact, one of the most powerful outcomes of using the business model frameworks (RTV, Lean, OBMC) with a non-traditional organisation is the requirement to clarify key elements such as value creation, customer need and key resources.

You might find yourself using business model thinking to assess a variety of non-business organisations: educational institutions, governmental entities, non-profit foundations, NGOs, community groups, online forums. What is the business model of the United Nations? FIFA? MI6? The Girl Scouts? What 'value' does each of these entities create? Who is the customer and what is the need? What are the key resources that make it possible for each of these entities to create and capture value?

Back to business model basics: what to remember from this book

In the final analysis, our business model journey covered four key topics: what business models are (and are not), the elements that comprise business models, useful tools for business model analysis and a cycle for evaluating and changing business models with an eye towards sustainability.

Ultimately, a business model is a design exemplified by a map or a story. It describes a set of organisational elements and how those elements work together. Those elements are centred on resources, transactions and value creation. When those elements are coherent, working together to generate a consistent and compelling narrative, then the business model may be viable. We can use various canvases and frameworks to describe, explore, evaluate and change business models. Ultimately, we know that business models have to be tested in the real world; there are no business model guarantees!

We have added a new type of innovation, business model innovation, to our repertoire of organisational change. We can think more clearly about how and why business models may be sustainable. As entrepreneurs, managers, trustees, shareholders and consumers, we can choose to apply a more holistic approach to value creation that incorporates long-term ecological and social benefits.

Every day, we work with entrepreneurs striving to create change. Some will succeed; some will fail. Some change will be focused on maximising profits; some change will strive to improve the world. Some will use old, proven business models to create sustainable and trustworthy organisations. Some will generate entirely new business models that change companies, industries and even society.

Through complexity and confusion, business models provide a powerful and insightful tool for exploring opportunities.

Where will your business model journey take you?

'By simply capitalizing on core strengths and knowledge, companies and entrepreneurs can engage in an emerging business model that will enable them to create – and demonstrate – real, sustainable social impact in society.'

Muhammad Yunnus

RECAP

- A business model is a design that ties together resources, transactions and value creation.
- Business model analysis is the single best indicator for whether an organisation is viable.
- Business models must be tested: we cannot always predict why some business models work and others do not.
- Business model innovation is a high-risk, high-reward process.
- Successful business models reflect the norms and values of the broader socio-economic context: business models are not required to be nice.

References

As of September 2017, searching Google Scholar for 'business model' returns nearly 600,000 hits. Clearly, there is no possible references list that comprehensively covers the academic and practice literatures of business models. The list below is designed for one specific purpose: to give the interested reader an accessible starting point for learning more about business models. We have divided this list into 'Academic' and 'Practice' sections simply for convenience, based on our own arbitrary sense of whether a given publication more obviously appeals to academics or practitioners. This is our subjective take on key publications that can help a reader initiate a more thorough investigation. The thoughtful practitioner would benefit from many academic papers; the action-oriented academic does well to be aware of publications with direct impact on management practice. We hope the reader will indulge us for including our own contributions to this topic.

Academic

Bock, A. J., Opsahl, T., George, G., & Gann, D. M. (2012). The effects of culture and structure on strategic flexibility during business model innovation. Journal of Management Studies, 49(2), 279–305.

Chesbrough, H., & Rosenbloom, R. S. (2002). The role of the business model in capturing value from innovation: evidence from Xerox Corporation's technology spin-off companies. *Industrial and corporate change, 11(3),* 529–555.

Chesbrough, H. (2010). Business model innovation: opportunities and barriers. Long range planning, 43(2), 354–363.

DaSilva, C. M., & Trkman, P. (2014). Business model: what it is and what it is not. Long range planning, 47(6), 379–389.

Desyllas, P., Salter, A., & Oliver, A. (2017). When Does Business Model Reconfiguration Create Value?. Strategic Management Journal. George, G., & Bock, A. J. (2011). The business model in practice and its implications for entrepreneurship research. Entrepreneurship theory and practice, 35(1), 83–111.

Foss, N. J., & Saebi, T. (2017). Fifteen years of research on business model innovation: How far have we come, and where should we go?. Journal of Management, 43(1), 200–227.

Morris, M., Schindehutte, M., & Allen, J. (2005). The entrepreneur's business model: toward a unified perspective. Journal of business research, 58(6), 726–735.

Stubbs, W., & Cocklin, C. (2008). Conceptualizing a "sustainability business model". Organization & Environment, 21(2), 103–127.

Zott, C., & Amit, R. (2007). Business model design and the performance of entrepreneurial firms. Organization science, 18(2), 181–199.

Zott, C., & Amit, R. (2008). The fit between product market strategy and business model: implications for firm performance. Strategic management journal, 29(1), 1–26.

Zott, C., & Amit, R. (2010). Business model design: an activity system perspective. Long range planning, 43(2), 216–226.

Practice

Amit, R., & Zott, C. (2012). Creating value through business model innovation. MIT Sloan Management Review, 53(3), 41.

Bock, A. J., & George, G. (2014). Agile business model innovation. *European Business Review,* 8.

Casadesus-Masanell, R., & Ricart, J. E. (2011). How to design a winning business model. Harvard business review, 89(1/2), 100–107.

Chesbrough, H. (2007). Business model innovation: it's not just about technology anymore. Strategy & leadership, 35(6), 12–17.

Christensen, C. M., Bartman, T., & Van Bever, D. (2016). The hard truth about business model innovation. MIT Sloan Management Review, 58(1), 31.

Fernández, E., Montes, J. M., & Vázquez, C. J. (2000). Typology and strategic analysis of intangible resources: A resource-based approach. Technovation, 20(2), 81–92.

George, G., & Bock, A. J. (2012). Models of opportunity: How entrepreneurs design firms to achieve the unexpected. Cambridge University Press.

Giesen, E., Berman, S. J., Bell, R., & Blitz, A. (2007). Three ways to successfully innovate your business model. Strategy & leadership, 35(6), 27–33.

Johnson, M. W., Christensen, C. M., & Kagermann, H. (2008). Reinventing your business model. *Harvard business review,* 86(12), 57–68.

Magretta, J. (2002). Why business models matter.

Osterwalder, A., & Pigneur, Y. (2010). Business model generation: a handbook for visionaries, game changers, and challengers. John Wiley & Sons.

Weill, P., & Vitale, M. (2001). Place to space: Migrating to eBusiness Models. Harvard Business Press.

Index